Hidden Talent

Hidden Talent

How Leading Companies Hire, Retain, and Benefit from People with Disabilities

Edited by MARK L. LENGNICK-HALL

PRAEGER

Westport, Connecticut
London

Library of Congress Cataloging-in-Publication Data

Hidden talent : how leading companies hire, retain, and benefit from people with disabilities / edited by Mark L. Lengnick-Hall.

    p.   cm.

Includes bibliographical references and index.

ISBN 978–0–275–99289–7 (alk. paper)

1. People with disabilities—Employment—United States. 2. United States. Americans with Disabilities Act of 1990. 3. Discrimination against people with disabilities—United States. I. Lengnick-Hall, Mark L.

HD7256.U5.H53 2007

658.30087—dc22   2007000061

British Library Cataloguing in Publication Data is available.

Library of Congress Catalog Card Number: 2007000061

ISBN-13: 978–0–275–99289–7

ISBN-10: 0–275–99289–6

First published in 2007

Praeger Publishers, 88 Post Road West, Westport, CT 06881

An imprint of Greenwood Publishing Group, Inc.

www.praeger.com

Printed in the United States of America

The paper used in this book complies with the Permanent Paper Standard issued by the National Information Standards Organization (Z39.48–1984).

10 9 8 7 6 5 4 3 2 1

Contents

Preface*

Robert R. Hull

After over 25 years of research in assistive technology and workplace accommodations for people with disabilities, the Cerebral Palsy Research Foundation of Kansas decided as part of its strategic planning in 1998 to focus directly on employment research. Despite great gains in assistive technology, the Rehabilitation Act of 1978 and the Americans with Disabilities Act (ADA) of 1990, the employment rate for people with significant disabilities has stubbornly remained at only 25–33% during these years.

What are the factors influencing whether people with disabilities are hired and advanced in employment? We knew that even to begin to answer such a question would require a lengthy research agenda. First, we recognized that reliable and effective answers could only come from employers—that primary research was needed on the "demand" side of the labor equation, while most of the research done previously had focused on the "supply" side, preparing people with disabilities to be good job candidates, etc.

As a project team was developed including researchers from Wichita State University and the University of Texas at San Antonio, we sought out a key partner in the business world: the Society for Human Resource Management. Through their survey program, we were able to conduct a national Internet survey of 2,500 human resource managers. This survey gave us some answers—what these managers would say to survey questions.

* This research was part of the Employment Research and Organizational Development Project at the Cerebral Palsy Research Foundation of Kansas, supported by grants H133B010901, H235J020008, H235J030003, and H235J040008 from the U.S. Department of Education.

However, we knew that some topics were sensitive for employers, such as questions about lawsuits under the ADA, and whether being served by people with obvious disabilities was uncomfortable to their customers. So, we developed an innovative survey instrument to "get below" the easy answers. Together with DiscoverWhy, Inc., a market research company, we developed a recording of a "virtual focus group" (scripted to include our research questions and conducted by actors) of employers discussing their employees with disabilities. DiscoverWhy presented this as an audio-streamed recording over the Internet, and executives were asked to respond favorably or unfavorably to what they were hearing, using their computer mouse. DiscoverWhy was able to present us with a second-by-second tracing of these responses, separated out primarily by large, medium, and small companies in five economic sectors (manufacturing, distribution, information technology, retail sales, and financial services). By partnering with the National Association of Workforce Boards, we obtained a national sample of executives.

After analyzing the results of these two surveys, we approached a sample of 38 senior executives from companies across the country for 30–60-minute face-to-face interviews. In this way were able to probe more deeply into the most significant factors we had identified in the surveys. Washington, D.C., attorney John Kemp, well-known in both the business and disability communities, facilitated making the contacts we needed.

What became clear is that no single factor, or even small set of factors, was primary in the minds of business executives. What mattered was whether a solid business case could be made for employing people with disabilities. If the individual was productive, and added value to the workforce, these executives were confident other issues could be managed.

A labor economist on our project team undertook a review of the economic and management literature on the topic, and then conducted an economic impact study of Center Industries Corporation, a midwestern manufacturing company whose workforce included an average of 46% employees with disabilities over the five years of the study. Results showed both sustained revenue growth by the company over that period and significant decreases in financial supports from federal and state agencies by their employees with disabilities.

Clearly, a business case could be made. Center Industries Corporation was one proactive example. We asked ourselves: Are there other proactive companies, what motivated them, and what changes and results have they experienced? What could be learned from their successes and their remaining challenges? Those questions led us toward case studies; in order to be consistent with our earlier research, we sought to identify widely recognized proactive companies of different sizes and in different economic sectors. We began with companies that had received the New Freedom Initiative Award in 2002–2004 from the U.S. Department of Labor, and added others from groups such as the Business Leadership Network and the National Disability and Business Council. The seven case studies in this book are from this research.

Our hope is that this book will contribute to the knowledge base and the motivation of business executives and managers on the one hand, and rehabilitation professionals on the other, to make the national labor market one that works for people with disabilities. An employment rate for them of 33% or less can simply no longer be acceptable. Our society can no longer afford to overlook this hidden talent.

Introduction

Mark L. Lengnick-Hall

You probably know someone with a disability. You may even have a disability yourself. Some disabilities are noticeable, such as someone confined to a wheelchair because of cerebral palsy. Other disabilities are not noticeable at all. That person next to you at work, whom you do not think of as having a disability because you cannot see it, may actually have one—either physical or mental. Moreover, even if you don't have a disability now—and you live long enough—you probably will acquire one as a result of the aging process. The National Organization on Disability reports that the likelihood of experiencing a disability increases with age, with disability rates of 1.7% among those aged less than 22, 6.4% among those aged 22–44, 11.5% among those aged 45–54, 21.9% among those aged 55–64, 27.8% among those aged 65–79, and 53.5% among those over 80.[1] And, because many disabilities are due to accidents, any nondisabled person, regardless of age, could acquire one virtually at any time, such as becoming paralyzed from a car accident.

For something as seemingly ubiquitous as disabilities, it is surprising that so many people are so uninformed about them. This is especially true when it comes to the employment arena. Countless websites and brochures address myths and stereotypes about people with disabilities and their ability to function effectively in business organizations. If the general public were better informed, there would be no need for such myth- and stereotype-busters. It is not surprising then, that many employers are reluctant to hire people with disabilities.

This book is about companies that have discovered the hidden talent of people with disabilities. It is about how these companies hire, retain, and ultimately benefit from having people with disabilities in their workforces. It is about how other organizations can learn what steps to take in order to capitalize on the talents of people with disabilities.

WHAT IS A DISABILITY AND HOW PREVALENT ARE PEOPLE WITH DISABILITIES IN THE U.S. POPULATION?

What constitutes a disability is open to some debate.[2] However, legislation and case law in the U.S. has clarified—at least from a legal standpoint—the criteria for identifying a disability.[3] The Equal Employment Opportunity Commission (EEOC) defines disability as *both physical and mental impairments that substantially limit a major life activity of the person (e.g., breathing, walking, and working)*. This identifies in a rather technical way what the legal boundaries are for determining disability. The EEOC also defines someone as having a disability who has a record of impairment in the past or who is regarded by others as having such impairment. However, measures that can mitigate or correct the impairment (such as eyeglasses) must be taken into account in determining if someone has a disability. That is, impairment is assessed in its mitigated state. To clarify who is and who is not considered to have a disability, the EEOC provides the following definitions[4]:

1. Impairment is defined as "a physiological disorder affecting one or more of a number of body systems or a mental or psychological disorder." Excluded from the definition are: (1) environmental, cultural, and economic disadvantages; (2) homosexuality; (3) pregnancy; (4) physical characteristics; (5) common personality traits; and (6) normal deviations in height, weight, or strength.

2. Major life activities include "sitting, standing, lifting, and mental and emotional processes such as thinking, concentrating, and interacting with others."

3. Whether impairment is substantially limiting depends on its nature and severity, duration or expected duration, and its permanency or long-term impact (e.g., a broken arm or leg would not be considered a disability).

4. To be substantially limiting, the impairment must prevent or significantly restrict the individual from performing a class of jobs or a broad range of jobs in various classes (e.g., an impairment that prevented the individual from performing only a single job likely would not be considered a

disability, nor would an impairment that kept an individual from performing just certain tasks on a particular job).

5. A mental impairment includes mental or emotional illness (e.g., depres-
   sion, bipolar disorder). To count as a mental disability, the mental impairment must substantially limit one or more of the major life activities.

The definition of disability used by the American Community Survey (a
survey of the U.S. Census Bureau designed to replace the decennial census
long form) is based on three questions[5]:

1. Does this person have any of the following long-lasting conditions:
   (a) blindness, deafness, or a severe vision or hearing impairment? and
   (b) a condition that substantially limits one or more basic physical activities such as walking, climbing stairs, reaching, lifting, or carrying?

2. Because of a physical, mental, or emotional condition lasting 6 months or
   more, does this person have any difficulty in doing any of the following
   activities: (a) learning, remembering, or concentrating? and (b) dressing,
   bathing, or getting around inside the home?

3. Because of a physical, mental, or emotional condition lasting 6 months or
   more, does this person have any difficulty in doing any of the following
   activities: (a) going outside the home alone to shop or visit a doctor's
   office? (b) working at a job or business?

The 2000 Census counted 49.7 million people with some type of lasting
condition or disability.[6] Therefore, people with disabilities represented 19.3%
of the 257.2 million people who were aged 5 and older in the civilian noninstitutionalized population. That means *nearly one person in five in the U.S. has
a disability*.

DO PEOPLE WITH DISABILITIES WANT TO WORK
AND DO THEY MAKE GOOD EMPLOYEES?

Most people with disabilities want to work. Sixty-seven percent of people
with disabilities who are unemployed say they would prefer to be working.
That is, two out of three unemployed people with disabilities would prefer to be
working.[7] And, people with disabilities have human capital, such as education,
that is valuable to employers. In fact, according to the National Organization
on Disability/Harris poll, 72% of working-age people with disabilities have

high school diplomas or a higher education. However, of those with a college degree, 55% are unemployed, compared to 14% of college-educated people without disabilities.[8]

People with disabilities make good employees. Research studies dating back to 1948 have consistently shown that employees with disabilities have average or better attendance, lower turnover, and average or better job performance, and average or better safety records than their nondisabled counterparts.[9] Furthermore, insurance costs do not rise appreciably for employees with disabilities in contrast to nondisabled employees. And, the cost of accommodations for most employers is quite small relative to the benefits gained. The Job Accommodation Network (JAN) has conducted a survey on the cost of accommodation since October 1992. JAN surveys employers who call for accommodation information to obtain feedback on the cost and benefit of accommodation. Results indicate that 71% of accommodations cost $500 or less, with 20% of those costing nothing.[10] If you think about the cost of accommodation similar to a signing bonus for a highly desired employee, it is a small price to pay.

WHY DON'T EMPLOYERS HIRE MORE PEOPLE WITH DISABILITIES?

There are a number of reasons why employers don't hire people with disabilities—some based on valid concerns, some based on ignorance, some based on prejudice and stereotypes, and some based on historical precedence. The Industrial Revolution that led to the development of modern-day corporations had its roots in manufacturing and the creation of jobs in plants that placed a premium on physical ability. Early assembly lines required long hours of arduous work and were not forgiving to employees who had disabilities or acquired disabilities on the job, such as from industrial accidents. Consequently, organizations evolved over time to favor the nondisabled over people with disabilities. Jobs, processes, and other aspects of the workplace were designed around people who did not have disabilities. It was probably a natural result that both managers and workers developed attitudes and opinions that people with disabilities could not perform most jobs in most organizations.

Many negative attitudes and stereotypes regarding people with disabilities persist even today.[11] For example, employers may believe that people with disabilities will cost more in health insurance claims, have more accidents at work, be less productive than nondisabled workers, and even be more likely to sue over discrimination claims. Ignorance, misunderstanding, and lack of imagination are the likely culprits in creating a hostile environment for people with disabilities in the workplace. While laws such as the Americans with Disabilities (ADA) have gone a long way toward remedying workplace discrimination against people with disabilities, changing attitudes of managers and workers has proved more difficult and slow. That is why organizations, such as those profiled in this book, can provide leadership in shattering myths and stereotypes and demonstrating how hiring people with disabilities can be a sound business decision.

Employers seem to take three approaches to people with disabilities: ignore, comply, or value. Those employers that choose the first strategy—the ignore approach—simply do not pay attention to the issue of hiring people with disabilities. They favor nondisabled applicants over applicants with disabilities and take their chances with possible litigation. Of course the potential costs of such a strategy include getting sued for discrimination, loss of reputation in the community resulting from bad publicity, and perhaps loss of customers with disabilities who find other companies with whom to do business.

A second strategy focuses on compliance. Employers who choose this approach pay attention to legal requirements and ensure that they follow the law. They do not actively seek out employees with disabilities, but neither do they discourage them from applying for jobs. If implemented well, this approach will minimize costs associated with litigation and bad press, but possibly miss out on the benefits that could be obtained from actively seeking out people with disabilities for employment. Costs of compliance, such as building accessibility and job accommodations, are borne by all organizations, so compliance yields no competitive advantage.

The third strategy focuses on valuing people with disabilities. Going beyond mere compliance, employers who choose this approach seek out people with disabilities and create organizational cultures and climates that are disability-friendly. The costs associated with this approach are small in comparison to the benefits obtained, such as acquiring the most talented employees—many of whom have disabilities. This strategy can actually lead to a competitive advantage, since other companies who do not proactively recruit from the pool of applicants with disabilities limit their access to the best talent.

The Research behind This Book

This book is about companies that choose the third approach described above: valuing people with disabilities. The companies profiled in this book are leaders in hiring and retaining people with disabilities. This book is based upon a case study research program that involved three institutions: the Cerebral Palsy Research Foundation of Wichita, Kansas; Wichita State University; and the University of Texas at San Antonio. We used a case study approach because we were interested in discovering the variety of programs, practices, and policies used by companies to attract and retain people with disabilities. The companies included in this study were chosen as extreme or unique cases since many—if not most—organizations do not make such proactive efforts toward hiring PWDs. Our goal was to identify programs, practices, and policies that may be effectively used to hire and retain PWDs and provide initial foundations for future research and practice.

Seven companies recognized for their proactive programs, policies, and practices—and success in employing people with disabilities—were identified for this research. The companies who participated in this research included: Microsoft Corporation (Redmond, Washington), SunTrust Bank (Richmond, Virginia), Dow Chemical Corporation (Midland, Michigan), Marriott Foundation for Disabilities (Atlanta, Georgia), Hewlett-Packard (Palo Alto, California),Giant Eagle Supermarkets (Pittsburgh, Pennsylvania), and A. & F. Wood Products (Howell, Michigan). The studies were conducted with the companies in 2005 and present accurate information from that time. For current information, please visit each company's website.

Six of these companies had been winners in the previous three competitions conducted by the U.S. Department of Labor for its New Freedom Initiative Award. The Secretary of Labor's New Freedom Initiative Award annually recognizes non-profits, small businesses, corporations, and individuals that have demonstrated exemplary and innovative efforts in furthering the employment and workplace environment for people with disabilities.[12]

THE PURPOSE OF THIS BOOK

The purpose of this book is to describe how leading companies hire and retain people with disabilities so that other companies can follow their lead. One goal is to understand the range of policies, practices, and procedures used to hire and retain people with disabilities. Another goal is to synthesize and integrate the information in order to develop some guidelines for practice that other companies can use.

The intended audience for this book primarily is executives, human resource managers, and general managers—those who think about, plan, develop strategies, and take action in companies regarding how human resources are utilized. Secondarily we believe that rehabilitation professionals, consultants, academics, students, and others also will find this book useful. Hopefully this book will open eyes to an untapped and valuable human resource—people with disabilities.

PLAN OF THE BOOK

A brief overview of each chapter is provided next. The book is organized into three main sections.

Section 1—The Problem and the Opportunity: People with Disabilities Need Jobs and Employers Need Workers consists of two chapters.

- *Chapter 1* describes demographic and labor market trends that make hiring people with disabilities a good human resource strategy for the future. The retirements of baby boom generation employees in the next ten to fifteen years coupled with a smaller replacement labor pool will place demands on employers. People with disabilities represent a largely untapped labor pool that can be used to meet these demands.
- *Chapter 2* reviews the literature on why employers don't hire people with disabilities as well as common employer myths and misperceptions about people with disabilities. Many employers lack sufficient relevant information about people with disabilities and the potential contributions they could make and consequently ignore this valuable source of labor—even during good economic times when labor is hard to obtain.

Section 2—Solutions: What Some Leading Companies Are Doing to Hire and Retain People with Disabilities consists of seven chapters.

- *Chapter 3* describes how Hewlett-Packard incorporates people with disabilities into their workforce. This company has been actively involved in recruiting persons with disabilities through partnerships with a variety of organizations, schools, and other external networks. Internally, it has made numerous workplace accommodations for its employees with disabilities and has encouraged and supported affinity groups. In general, the company focuses on making its own products accessible to people with disabilities and partners with others to create and distribute assistive technologies. It involves persons with disabilities in the development of accessibility guidelines and in the design and testing of products and services.

- *Chapter 4* describes how, as a multinational company, Dow Chemical creates opportunities for people with disabilities on a global basis. When functioning in Germany, for example, Dow must employ 5% of its workforce from among persons with disabilities; when functioning in the United States, it must meet the Americans with Disabilities Act standards for accessibility of its facilities. Dow has taken the approach that it will seek the most stringent standards worldwide, and incorporate those standards into its strategic planning everywhere else. This enables Dow to bid and compete globally, without being slowed by sudden efforts to meet higher standards.

- *Chapter 5* describes SunTrust Bank, a major financial institution on the U.S. east coast that uses Disability Councils to be responsive to employees with disabilities. Their councils are composed of selected and appointed representative employees (rather than being an affinity group of self-selected employees). Incorporating persons with disabilities into visible positions at all levels has proven to be a good marketing strategy; for example, one branch manager who is blind found that many other blind customers went out of their way to conduct business at her branch because of assistance they received there, and that became known in their community's population of blind persons, leading to significant revenue growth.

- *Chapter 6* describes a unique small company that has totally integrated persons with disabilities into its workforce. This company, which is located in Howell, Michigan, and which specializes in the manufacture of wood doors and frames, has 20 employees, 7 (35%) of whom have some kind of disability. Initially, some ten years ago, the company hired a person with a disability because there was a shortage of qualified labor. Since then, this employee has worked so effectively that the managers have systematically sought other persons with disabilities as employees, and the business now has developed a distinct culture in which the work of these individuals is highly prized. The workshop foreman has developed specific accommodations for specific disabilities, which has not only speeded production but also allowed employees to take pride in their productivity.

- *Chapter 7* describes Giant Eagle Supermarkets, headquartered in Pittsburgh, Pennsylvania, with approximately 200 stores in Pennsylvania, West Virginia, Maryland, and Ohio. Giant Eagle strongly follows the supported employment approach, with community rehabilitation organizations providing job coaches to assist new employees with disabilities. Community organizations are a significant part of Giant Eagle's marketing strategies, with discounts offered for purchase of shopping certificates that rebate a portion to the nonprofit. When Giant Eagle lost a court case on an employee disability issue, the community rallied around to point out publicly what a proactive employer they were.

- *Chapter 8* describes Microsoft, a multinational company with more of its revenues coming from overseas than from the United States. Microsoft uses employee disability councils rather than affinity groups. It has integrated its disability employment policies into its human resource policies for training. When a new employee or, in one case, even a summer intern with a disability is brought in, the entire work team is expected to participate in training to most efficiently accommodate the new worker. In the case of the summer intern, 19 team members took classes for 1.5 hours a week for 10 weeks to learn American Sign Language (ASL). Now other employees have asked to take the ASL course after-hours in order to learn how to communicate with their infant children who are pre-verbal.

- *Chapter 9* describes the Marriott Foundation, which operates the "Bridges Program," which focuses on entry-level employment for low-income young people, including youth with disabilities. While the Foundation is structurally independent from Marriott Hotels, the latter has been a very proactive employer of persons with disabilities in its nationwide network of hotels. The foundation and the hotel corporation both make strong efforts to see that acceptance of disability in both the workplace and in serving its customers with disabilities is a proactive part of the company culture.

Section 3—Lessons Learned about Hiring and Retaining People with Disabilities consists of three chapters.

- *Chapter 10* describes how companies can make a business case for hiring people with disabilities. Typically, arguments made for hiring people with disabilities focus on the social desirability of doing so, with an implication that businesses incur greater costs than benefits. Recent research suggests that companies can gain a competitive advantage through hiring a diverse workforce.

- *Chapter 11* describes proven methods for creating an organizational culture that is receptive to hiring and retaining people with disabilities. Examples from the seven cases in Section 2 are used to illustrate major organizational change principles that any organization can use to improve its ability to hire and retain people with disabilities.

- *Chapter 12* ties the three sections together and draws some general conclusions about what has been learned from research and corporate practice about hiring people with disabilities.

Appendixes. There are four appendixes.

- *Appendix 1* provides detailed information about tax incentives available to employers for hiring people with disabilities.
- *Appendix 2* provides sources of information readers can consult for further information about hiring people with disabilities.
- *Appendix 3* describes the Cerebral Palsy Research Foundation that supported the research program described in this book.
- *Appendix 4* describes the basic elements of the Americans with Disabilities Act and how it affects employers.

The Problem and the Opportunity: People with Disabilities Need Jobs and Employers Need Workers

These two factors are also tied to the second trend that is likely to affect the workforce described below.

AGING POPULATION

The aging of the U.S. population is the second identified trend posed to dramatically affect the labor force in the first half of the 21st century. Birth rates fluctuated in the United States during the 20th century leading to a relatively large aging group of Americans in the early 21st century. In the first two decades of the 20th century, both high rates of reproduction and relatively high levels of immigration from Europe occurred. This was followed by a "birth dearth" in the late 1920s and early 1930s. This birth dearth has resulted in what will be a slow growth rate of the 75 and older group in the first decade of the 21st century. Beginning in 1946 and ending in 1964, the well-known "baby boom" led to a surge in the birth rate and population level. It is not surprising that this group aging will lead to the 55- to 64-year-old range to have the greatest growth rate (an increase of 11.5 million) in the first 12 years of the 21st century. Thus, the baby boomer generation aging and enjoying an increase in their life expectancy is one of the driving forces of the graying of the American population. Furthermore, the U.S. fertility rates have decreased since the birth of the baby boomer generation. The "baby bust" followed the baby boom with a decrease in birthrates until the mid-1970s. This translates to a 3.8 million reduction in the U.S. population falling in the 35–44 age range. As the baby boomers came of age and started to have their own children, the "baby boom echo" resulted in a modest increase in births. As a result, the share of the population over 65 is expected to reach 13% this decade. The share of the population over 65 is expected to grow to 20% in 2050 and 23% by 2100.

IMMIGRATION

The third factor identified as having a significant impact on the population is immigration. The share of immigration in the U.S. population growth has steadily increased since the 1930s. Since the 1990s immigrants have supplied approximately 35% of the growth in the nation's population. Immigrants had not made up such a large proportion of population growth in the United States since the early 1900s. New immigrants and their offspring are expected to account for almost two-thirds of the growth in the U.S. population between

CHAPTER 1

Where Will Businesses Find the Workers They Need in the Future?

Jodi Messer Pelkowski

Considerable attention has been given to the changing demographic and labor market trends in the United States. The aging of the population coupled with falling fertility rates have led to a decrease in the growth of labor supply. In essence, retirements of baby boom generation employees in the next 10–15 years, coupled with a smaller replacement labor pool, will place significant demands on employers looking to fill job openings. People with disabilities represent a largely untapped labor pool that can be used to alleviate this problem.

HOW THE LABOR FORCE IS MEASURED

Given the labor force of a country is comprised mostly of its own people, it is not surprising that changes in the general population will trigger changes in its labor force. The labor force refers to the portion of the population aged 16 or older either working or actively seeking work, or expecting recall from a layoff. The labor force participation rate is the labor force as a percentage of the 16 and older noninstitutionalized population. Two factors drive the change in the labor force: population growth and labor force participation rates. Population will change with changes in fertility rates, mortality rates, and immigration. Labor force participation rates are often influenced by changes in the social and political climate. When experts forecast or predict changes in the labor force they look to changes in population and labor force participation rates. A review of the changes in the population, labor force participation rates, and labor force is helpful in understanding the future projections of the labor force.

THREE LABOR MARKET TRENDS

It is expected that the U.S. population will grow more slowly in the 21st century than in previous extended periods of time. As noted above, three main demographic trends are likely to produce some major shifts in the labor market. Two of the demographic trends, a decline in the growth of the U.S. population and the aging of the population, are likely to lead to a shrinking labor force. The third trend, a surge in immigration, can help to offset the decrease in the labor force. Furthermore, immigration will lead to changes in the skill level of the workforce; specifically in terms of educational attainment.[1] While other economists have looked at each of these trends separately, Jane Sneddon Little and Robert K. Triest, two economists at the Federal Reserve Bank of Boston, examined the impact of all three of these projected trends on the U.S. labor market. They note with some wonder how a shrinking labor force will be able to meet the consumption needs of the nation and maintain the nation's standard of living.

SLOW LABOR FORCE GROWTH

The Census Bureau and Bureau of Labor Statistics release medium-term, or 10-year, projections of population and labor force every 2 years. In addition, Mitra Toossi, an economist at the Bureau of Labor Statistics, reports on the historical and projected changes in the labor force for the years 1950–2050. According to the Census Bureau's most recent middle series projection,* the annual growth rate of the U.S. population is expected to decrease over the first half of the 21st century. As can be seen in   Figure 1.1, the annual growth rate has steadily declined in the second half of the 20th century. In the 1950s, the annual growth rate was between 1.5% and 1.75%. By the 1990s, the population grew at a slower rate of 1% per year. The Census Bureau predicts the gradual descent to continue to approximately 0.7% annual growth in population by 2050. According to Little and Triest, the decline in the population growth can be attributed to two factors: a rise in the death rate as the population ages and a fall in birth rates as a share of the childbearing population decreases.

---

*The Census Bureau provides three series of projections. The middle series projection is designated as the most likely outcome predicted by the Census Bureau. The high and low series are also provided to demonstrate the upper and lower bounds, or measures of the degree of uncertainty surrounding the middle projection (U.S. Census Bureau).

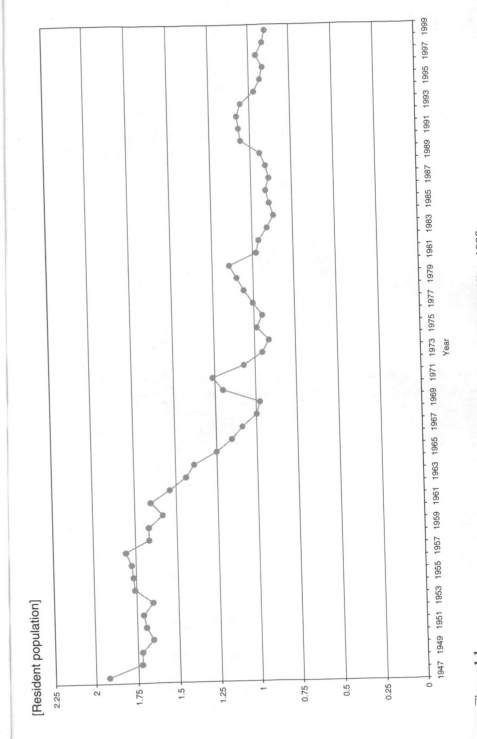

Total Population of the United States, 1947 to 1999

1998 and 2100 according to the Census Bureau's middle series projection. The Census Bureau expects the immigration flows to be largely from Mexico and other countries in Central and Latin America. Immigration is the most difficult component of population growth to project. Data from the Census 2000 suggests that the Census Bureau underestimated the growth of the population by 2% over the 10-year period between 1990 and 2000. This decade saw the largest gain (13.2%) in population since the 1960s. The Hispanic population grew by 3 million more than the Census Bureau projected. This accounts for almost half of the unexpected 2% increase in the U.S. population for 1990–2000.[2]

CHANGES IN LABOR FORCE PARTICIPATION

We have established that the population growth is expected to steadily decrease in the first half of the century. Furthermore, the population is aging while fertility rates are decreasing, leading to those of working age making up a smaller share of the population. This leads us to the other factor that influences the size of the labor force, the labor force participation rate.

According to Mitra Toossi, the civilian labor force grew from 62 million in 1950 to 141 million in 2000. This translates to a 1.6% annual growth rate. Toossi reports the population growth accounted for the growth rate of the labor force during the 1950s and 1960s. During the late 1970s and 1980s, population growth accounted for three-fourths of the labor force growth, with the remaining increase in the labor force growth due to increases in the labor force participation.[3]

Women had much to do with the changes in the labor force participation rate and, therefore, the growth of the U.S. labor force in the second half of the 20th century. In 1950, just slightly over one-third of the U.S. labor force consisted of women. The U.S. economy experienced an expansion for the two decades following World War II. Economic growth spurred an increase in demand for labor as productivity and the standard of living rose. The postwar era was a time when college enrollments and education attainment grew considerably. At the same time, the women's rights movement and legislation promoting equal opportunity in employment started to change society's view on women working outside the home.[4] These changes led to a particularly rapid increase in the labor force participation of women during the mid-1960s to late 1970s (see Figure 1.2). This also corresponds with the entrance of the baby boomer generation into the labor market. The growth continued through the 1980s but has since leveled out in the 1990s. The labor force participation rate of women

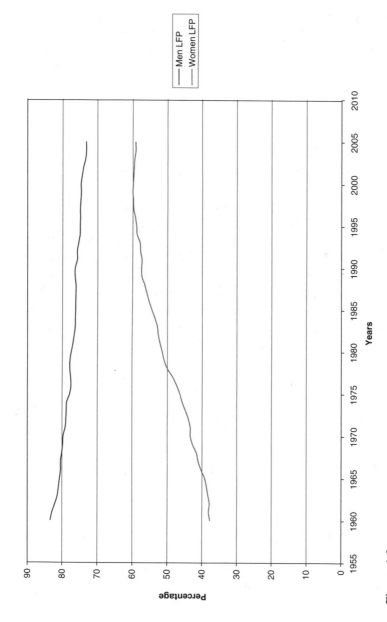

Figure 1.2
U. S. Labor Force Participation Rates
Source: **Bureau of Labor Statistics, U.S. Census Bureau.**

has hovered around 60%. While the labor force participation of women has stabilized at a rate quite lower than males, it is difficult to foresee a large change in the labor force participation of women in the labor force. By 2000, women made up almost 47% of the workforce.[5] Toossi projects the labor force participation to peak at 62% around the year 2010 but then decline slowly to 57% in 2050. She explains that the participation rate of younger females is not expected to change much; however, the aging females are expected to phase into retirement.[6]

During the latter half of the 20th century, males' labor force participation had slowly declined. While the labor force participation of males was over 80% in the 1950s and 1960s, it has slowly declined since then. By 2000, the labor force participation rate of males fell to approximately 75%. The decline in the participation rate for males is projected to continue reaching 67% by 2050.[7]

A TIGHT LABOR MARKET IN THE COMING DECADES

The two factors that drive the changes in the size of the labor force—population growth and labor force participation—both suggest a slowdown in the growth rate in the labor force. While the United States experienced growth rates of 1–1.75% in the latter half of the 20th century, it is projected that the first half of the 21st century will encounter a lower growth rate of 0.6% annually. The Hudson Institute's report *Workforce 2020: Work and Workers in the 21st Century* concludes the United States will face a tight labor market in the coming decades.**

It will be interesting to see how the economy reacts to a shrinking supply of labor. A dramatic decrease in the growth rate of the labor force could bring about a variety of changes. Peter McDonald and Rebecca Kippen note that the aging population and reduction in labor force growth is not unique to the United States, but rather is a phenomenon many advanced countries will face. In their study of 16 developed countries, they conclude that if current demographic and labor force trends continue, many of the countries will face either stagnation or a decline in the size of the labor force. In fact, they project

---

** A labor market is considered tight when jobs in general are plentiful and hard for employers to fill. In these times, the unemployed are likely to find jobs with relative ease and the unemployment rate is relatively low. On the other hand, a loose labor market is marked by employers filling jobs with relative ease but workers are abundant and face a relatively high unemployment rate. It is expected that the labor market will become tighter in the next 10-15 years.

that the United States is more likely than almost any other developed country to experience growth in their future labor supply.[8]

According to McDonald and Kippen, while projections of labor supply are relatively robust, labor demand is very difficult to project in the long run. Businesses may look toward new technology and capital investments aimed at increasing labor productivity. Producers will have an incentive to substitute equipment and labor-saving technological or organizational improvements if labor becomes scarce. Economists expect growth in labor productivity as the supply or growth rate of supply declines.[9] Furthermore, shifts in the composition of goods and services demanded may displace some workers.

WHERE WILL BUSINESSES FIND WORKERS?

If businesses cannot find workers in the United States, it is plausible they may look to find labor elsewhere. Thus, outsourcing or moving production offshore may become even more prevalent. However, if McDonald and Kippen are correct in their projections of a shrinking labor force being a global issue, moving offshore may not be a practical alternative.

To overcome a shrinking labor force due to the aging population and lower fertility rates, an alternative is to adopt a policy aimed at increasing the labor force participation rate of a country's population. As the authors of *Workforce 2020* point out, many factors influence labor force participation. Social insurance programs and the level of education of the workforce are of particular interest in the face of the current aging workforce. More educated or higher skilled workers typically remain in the labor force longer than lower skilled and less educated workers. With the increase in education levels beginning with the baby boomers, workers in professional occupations may be enticed to remain in the labor market in later ages. The real value of retirement benefits such as Social Security and Medicare can also influence participation rates. If the benefits (in real terms) of either program decline, older workers will have an incentive to remain in the labor market. Policies such as The Senior Citizens Freedom to Work Act enacted in 2000 which eliminated the "earnings limit" of workers aged 60–70 also could be used as incentive to keep older workers in the workforce.[10] If baby boomers continue to work as they get older, one probable consequence is more of them will acquire disabilities and require accommodations in the workplace.

Little and Triest, concerned with the rising dependency ratio (the ratio of those under 15 and over 65 to the working-age population), look back to the adjustments made during the 1960s. With the relatively large number

CHAPTER 1

Where Will Businesses Find the Workers They Need in the Future?

Jodi Messer Pelkowski

Considerable attention has been given to the changing demographic and labor market trends in the United States. The aging of the population coupled with falling fertility rates have led to a decrease in the growth of labor supply. In essence, retirements of baby boom generation employees in the next 10–15 years, coupled with a smaller replacement labor pool, will place significant demands on employers looking to fill job openings. People with disabilities represent a largely untapped labor pool that can be used to alleviate this problem.

HOW THE LABOR FORCE IS MEASURED

Given the labor force of a country is comprised mostly of its own people, it is not surprising that changes in the general population will trigger changes in its labor force. The labor force refers to the portion of the population aged 16 or older either working or actively seeking work, or expecting recall from a layoff. The labor force participation rate is the labor force as a percentage of the 16 and older noninstitutionalized population. Two factors drive the change in the labor force: population growth and labor force participation rates. Population will change with changes in fertility rates, mortality rates, and immigration. Labor force participation rates are often influenced by changes in the social and political climate. When experts forecast or predict changes in the labor force they look to changes in population and labor force participation rates. A review of the changes in the population, labor force participation rates, and labor force is helpful in understanding the future projections of the labor force.

THREE LABOR MARKET TRENDS

It is expected that the U.S. population will grow more slowly in the 21st century than in previous extended periods of time. As noted above, three main demographic trends are likely to produce some major shifts in the labor market. Two of the demographic trends, a decline in the growth of the U.S. population and the aging of the population, are likely to lead to a shrinking labor force. The third trend, a surge in immigration, can help to offset the decrease in the labor force. Furthermore, immigration will lead to changes in the skill level of the workforce; specifically in terms of educational attainment.[1] While other economists have looked at each of these trends separately, Jane Sneddon Little and Robert K. Triest, two economists at the Federal Reserve Bank of Boston, examined the impact of all three of these projected trends on the U.S. labor market. They note with some wonder how a shrinking labor force will be able to meet the consumption needs of the nation and maintain the nation's standard of living.

SLOW LABOR FORCE GROWTH

The Census Bureau and Bureau of Labor Statistics release medium-term, or 10-year, projections of population and labor force every 2 years. In addition, Mitra Toossi, an economist at the Bureau of Labor Statistics, reports on the historical and projected changes in the labor force for the years 1950–2050. According to the Census Bureau's most recent middle series projection,* the annual growth rate of the U.S. population is expected to decrease over the first half of the 21st century. As can be seen in Figure 1.1, the annual growth rate has steadily declined in the second half of the 20th century. In the 1950s, the annual growth rate was between 1.5% and 1.75%. By the 1990s, the population grew at a slower rate of 1% per year. The Census Bureau predicts the gradual descent to continue to approximately 0.7% annual growth in population by 2050. According to Little and Triest, the decline in the population growth can be attributed to two factors: a rise in the death rate as the population ages and a fall in birth rates as a share of the childbearing population decreases.

---

*The Census Bureau provides three series of projections. The middle series projection is designated as the most likely outcome predicted by the Census Bureau. The high and low series are also provided to demonstrate the upper and lower bounds, or measures of the degree of uncertainty surrounding the middle projection (U.S. Census Bureau).

[Resident population]

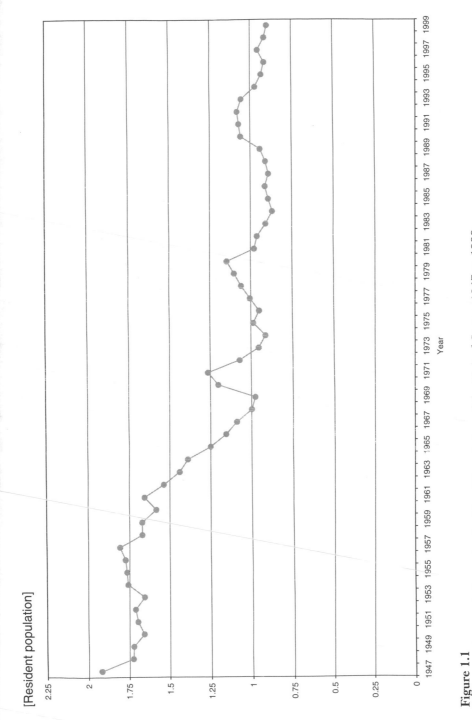

Year

Figure 1.1
The Annual Growth Rates for the Total Population of the United States, 1947 to 1999
Source: U.S. Census Bureau http://www.census.gov/population/documentation/twps0050/graphs.xls

These two factors are also tied to the second trend that is likely to affect the workforce described below.

AGING POPULATION

The aging of the U.S. population is the second identified trend posed to dramatically affect the labor force in the first half of the 21st century. Birth rates fluctuated in the United States during the 20th century leading to a relatively large aging group of Americans in the early 21st century. In the first two decades of the 20th century, both high rates of reproduction and relatively high levels of immigration from Europe occurred. This was followed by a "birth dearth" in the late 1920s and early 1930s. This birth dearth has resulted in what will be a slow growth rate of the 75 and older group in the first decade of the 21st century. Beginning in 1946 and ending in 1964, the well-known "baby boom" led to a surge in the birth rate and population level. It is not surprising that this group aging will lead to the 55- to 64-year-old range to have the greatest growth rate (an increase of 11.5 million) in the first 12 years of the 21st century. Thus, the baby boomer generation aging and enjoying an increase in their life expectancy is one of the driving forces of the graying of the American population. Furthermore, the U.S. fertility rates have decreased since the birth of the baby boomer generation. The "baby bust" followed the baby boom with a decrease in birthrates until the mid-1970s. This translates to a 3.8 million reduction in the U.S. population falling in the 35–44 age range. As the baby boomers came of age and started to have their own children, the "baby boom echo" resulted in a modest increase in births. As a result, the share of the population over 65 is expected to reach 13% this decade. The share of the population over 65 is expected to grow to 20% in 2050 and 23% by 2100.

IMMIGRATION

The third factor identified as having a significant impact on the population is immigration. The share of immigration in the U.S. population growth has steadily increased since the 1930s. Since the 1990s immigrants have supplied approximately 35% of the growth in the nation's population. Immigrants had not made up such a large proportion of population growth in the United States since the early 1900s. New immigrants and their offspring are expected to account for almost two-thirds of the growth in the U.S. population between

1998 and 2100 according to the Census Bureau's middle series projection. The Census Bureau expects the immigration flows to be largely from Mexico and other countries in Central and Latin America. Immigration is the most difficult component of population growth to project. Data from the Census 2000 suggests that the Census Bureau underestimated the growth of the population by 2% over the 10-year period between 1990 and 2000. This decade saw the largest gain (13.2%) in population since the 1960s. The Hispanic population grew by 3 million more than the Census Bureau projected. This accounts for almost half of the unexpected 2% increase in the U.S. population for 1990–2000.[2]

CHANGES IN LABOR FORCE PARTICIPATION

We have established that the population growth is expected to steadily decrease in the first half of the century. Furthermore, the population is aging while fertility rates are decreasing, leading to those of working age making up a smaller share of the population. This leads us to the other factor that influences the size of the labor force, the labor force participation rate.

According to Mitra Toossi, the civilian labor force grew from 62 million in 1950 to 141 million in 2000. This translates to a 1.6% annual growth rate. Toossi reports the population growth accounted for the growth rate of the labor force during the 1950s and 1960s. During the late 1970s and 1980s, population growth accounted for three-fourths of the labor force growth, with the remaining increase in the labor force growth due to increases in the labor force participation.[3]

Women had much to do with the changes in the labor force participation rate and, therefore, the growth of the U.S. labor force in the second half of the 20th century. In 1950, just slightly over one-third of the U.S. labor force consisted of women. The U.S. economy experienced an expansion for the two decades following World War II. Economic growth spurred an increase in demand for labor as productivity and the standard of living rose. The postwar era was a time when college enrollments and education attainment grew considerably. At the same time, the women's rights movement and legislation promoting equal opportunity in employment started to change society's view on women working outside the home.[4] These changes led to a particularly rapid increase in the labor force participation of women during the mid-1960s to late 1970s (see Figure 1.2). This also corresponds with the entrance of the baby boomer generation into the labor market. The growth continued through the 1980s but has since leveled out in the 1990s. The labor force participation rate of women

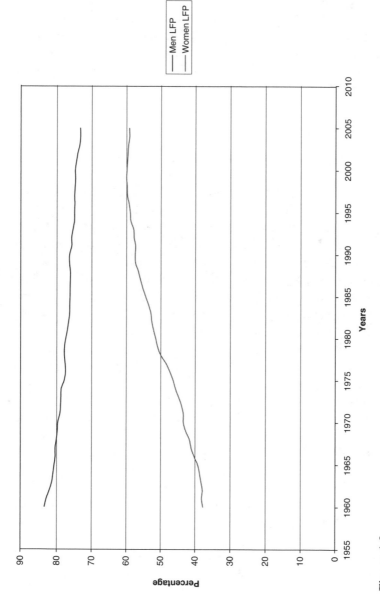

Figure 1.2
U. S. Labor Force Participation Rates
Source: **Bureau of Labor Statistics, U.S. Census Bureau.**

has hovered around 60%. While the labor force participation of women has stabilized at a rate quite lower than males, it is difficult to foresee a large change in the labor force participation of women in the labor force. By 2000, women made up almost 47% of the workforce.[5] Toossi projects the labor force participation to peak at 62% around the year 2010 but then decline slowly to 57% in 2050. She explains that the participation rate of younger females is not expected to change much; however, the aging females are expected to phase into retirement.[6]

During the latter half of the 20th century, males' labor force participation had slowly declined. While the labor force participation of males was over 80% in the 1950s and 1960s, it has slowly declined since then. By 2000, the labor force participation rate of males fell to approximately 75%. The decline in the participation rate for males is projected to continue reaching 67% by 2050.[7]

A TIGHT LABOR MARKET IN THE COMING DECADES

The two factors that drive the changes in the size of the labor force—population growth and labor force participation—both suggest a slowdown in the growth rate in the labor force. While the United States experienced growth rates of 1–1.75% in the latter half of the 20th century, it is projected that the first half of the 21st century will encounter a lower growth rate of 0.6% annually. The Hudson Institute's report *Workforce 2020: Work and Workers in the 21st Century* concludes the United States will face a tight labor market in the coming decades.**

It will be interesting to see how the economy reacts to a shrinking supply of labor. A dramatic decrease in the growth rate of the labor force could bring about a variety of changes. Peter McDonald and Rebecca Kippen note that the aging population and reduction in labor force growth is not unique to the United States, but rather is a phenomenon many advanced countries will face. In their study of 16 developed countries, they conclude that if current demographic and labor force trends continue, many of the countries will face either stagnation or a decline in the size of the labor force. In fact, they project

---

** A labor market is considered tight when jobs in general are plentiful and hard for employers to fill. In these times, the unemployed are likely to find jobs with relative ease and the unemployment rate is relatively low. On the other hand, a loose labor market is marked by employers filling jobs with relative ease but workers are abundant and face a relatively high unemployment rate. It is expected that the labor market will become tighter in the next 10-15 years.

that the United States is more likely than almost any other developed country to experience growth in their future labor supply.[8]

According to McDonald and Kippen, while projections of labor supply are relatively robust, labor demand is very difficult to project in the long run. Businesses may look toward new technology and capital investments aimed at increasing labor productivity. Producers will have an incentive to substitute equipment and labor-saving technological or organizational improvements if labor becomes scarce. Economists expect growth in labor productivity as the supply or growth rate of supply declines.[9] Furthermore, shifts in the composition of goods and services demanded may displace some workers.

WHERE WILL BUSINESSES FIND WORKERS?

If businesses cannot find workers in the United States, it is plausible they may look to find labor elsewhere. Thus, outsourcing or moving production offshore may become even more prevalent. However, if McDonald and Kippen are correct in their projections of a shrinking labor force being a global issue, moving offshore may not be a practical alternative.

To overcome a shrinking labor force due to the aging population and lower fertility rates, an alternative is to adopt a policy aimed at increasing the labor force participation rate of a country's population. As the authors of *Workforce 2020* point out, many factors influence labor force participation. Social insurance programs and the level of education of the workforce are of particular interest in the face of the current aging workforce. More educated or higher skilled workers typically remain in the labor force longer than lower skilled and less educated workers. With the increase in education levels beginning with the baby boomers, workers in professional occupations may be enticed to remain in the labor market in later ages. The real value of retirement benefits such as Social Security and Medicare can also influence participation rates. If the benefits (in real terms) of either program decline, older workers will have an incentive to remain in the labor market. Policies such as The Senior Citizens Freedom to Work Act enacted in 2000 which eliminated the "earnings limit" of workers aged 60–70 also could be used as incentive to keep older workers in the workforce.[10] If baby boomers continue to work as they get older, one probable consequence is more of them will acquire disabilities and require accommodations in the workplace.

Little and Triest, concerned with the rising dependency ratio (the ratio of those under 15 and over 65 to the working-age population), look back to the adjustments made during the 1960s. With the relatively large number of baby boomers entering retirement and being replaced with a smaller pool of workers, the dependency rate is projected to rise. In the early 2000s, the dependency ratio is just about 0.5. A steady increase in the dependency ratio to 0.67 in the early 2030s is expected to continue increasing to 0.72 in 2100. The early 1960s is somewhat comparable in that during this time the dependency ratio was relatively high. The baby boomers' entry into the labor market helped reduce the dependency ratio and keep the dependency ratio relatively low in historical terms.[11]

As discussed earlier, it is during the 1960s that the labor force participation for women began to climb. The entry of women and the increase in the labor force participation rate of women helped decrease the dependency rate and buoyed the supply of labor beginning in the 1960s. However, it is not likely that increases in the female labor force participation will occur again. Some might point to immigrants to fill the shoes that women filled in the 1960s. However, one aspect of the immigrant labor is much different from the women of the 1960s.

While immigration has the potential to help offset the slowing of the population growth, it also will likely impact the average level of education of the nation's workforce. The educational background of immigrants into the United States follows a bimodal pattern. Immigrants from Europe and Asia tend to have higher average education levels than the domestic population. However, migrants from Mexico and Latin America (the expected source of the majority of immigrants) tend to have less education than the U.S.-born population. While only 11% of the U.S.-born residents aged 25–64 have not completed high school, over two-thirds of Mexican immigrants in this same age range have not attained a high school education. It should be noted that children of immigrants take advantage of the U.S. educational system to attain much higher education levels, with less than one-third failing to graduate from high school. This trend is likely to pull down the average levels of education in the U.S. labor force.[12] Restructuring as a result of new technologies and the information technology age necessitate a skilled pool of workers.[13] Thus, immigrants may not have the skills required by the economy.

PEOPLE WITH DISABILITIES: AN UNTAPPED LABOR SOURCE

As businesses and government strive to replace the retiring baby boomer generation and deal with high dependency rates, an inward look to underutilized segments of the population may be necessary. Persons with disabilities are a relatively large group of potential workers businesses can look toward to fulfill their employment needs.

Based on the American Community Survey (as analyzed by researchers at Cornell University), here are some relevant statistics that describe the prevalence of people with disabilities in the labor force and the magnitude of their availability for meeting employer needs:[14]

1. In 2004—20,268,000 (12.1%) of the 167,902,000 working-age individuals reported one or more disabilities.

2. The employment rate of working-age people with disabilities decreased from 37.9% in 2003 to 37.5% in 2004, in the United States. Therefore, approximately 60% of working-age people with disabilities were not employed in 2004, in the United States.

3. The employment rate of working-age people without disabilities increased from 77.6% in 2003 to 77.8% in 2004, in the United States. Therefore, approximately 20% of working-age people without disabilities were not employed in 2004, in the United States.

4. The gap between the employment rates of working-age people with and without disabilities increased from 39.7% in 2003 to 40.3% in 2004, in the United States.

5. Of working-age people with disabilities, 22.4% are employed in full-time/full-year employment.

Therefore:

1. Of the approximately 20 million working-age people with disabilities,

    a. approximately 7.6 million are employed, and

    b. approximately 12.4 million are not employed.

2. Of the approximately 7.6 million working age people with disabilities who are employed,

    a. approximately 1.7 million are employed full-time/full-year, and

    b. approximately 5.9 million are employed part-time/part-year.

As you can see from the statistics, people with disabilities represent a large untapped source of labor in the United States. Organizations that can discover how to attract, retain, and benefit from hiring people with disabilities will be able both (1) to weather the upcoming shortage of labor as baby boomers begin to retire from the labor force and (2) gain a competitive advantage by obtaining valuable human capital overlooked by their competitors. The leading firms that we profile in our book are already reaping the benefits from talented people with disabilities.

CHAPTER 2

Why Employers Don't Hire People with Disabilities

Mark L. Lengnick-Hall and Philip Gaunt

Why don't employers hire more people with disabilities (PWDs)? To answer that question we identified six of the most commonly cited reasons employers don't hire PWDs and examined the research literature for each explanation. Our goal was to separate fact from myth and information from misinformation, and to provide a more objective analysis of employer concerns.

The following sections present the evidence for each potential barrier to employment for PWDs:

1. Employers don't hire PWDs because they lack necessary knowledge, skills, abilities, and other characteristics (KSAOs).

2. Employers don't hire PWDs because they have lower job performance and productivity than people without disabilities.

3. Employers don't hire PWDs because they entail higher costs than employees without disabilities.

4. Employers don't hire PWDs because they fear litigation associated with terminating PWDs.

5. Employers don't hire PWDs because of coworker reactions.

6. Employers don't hire PWDs because of customer reactions.

EXPLANATION 1: PWDs LACK NECESSARY KSAOs

One explanation for the low employment rate of PWDs is that they do not have the necessary KSAOs for job performance. Typical employer attitudes about whether PWDs have necessary KSAOs to perform jobs are mixed—some employers believe PWDs don't have the necessary skills and can't work; others view PWDs as punctual, hard-working, and competent.

What KSAOs do employers seek in potential employees and how do PWDs compare with people without disabilities? A recent study identified a limited number of generic behavioral descriptors used as selection factors across jobs (i.e., nonspecific KSAOs of desirable job candidates).[1] The KSAOs identified in the study included (a) *job knowledge/production skills*: knowledge, skills, and abilities that the worker has or develops on the job that affect his or her ability to get the job done—competencies directly related to performing job tasks; (b) *socialization and emotional coping skills*: social skills the worker has that affect his or her ability to get along with coworkers and supervisors and to cope with stress in the workplace; (c) *trainability/task flexibility*: academic and thinking skills a worker has that affect his or her ability to learn new skills and to be flexible in taking on new tasks; (d) *dependability*: behaviors that demonstrate accountability for time on task—competencies relating to being where you are supposed to be when you are supposed to be there; (e) *motivation/satisfaction*: behaviors that indicate commitment to and satisfaction with work—competencies related to job ownership, job satisfaction, and the willingness to exert effort in the performance of job tasks.

Direct comparisons between PWDs and people without disabilities across these KSAOs are incomplete, but suggestive. For example, while there are no direct data comparing the job knowledge of PWDs versus those without disabilities, there are data that suggest differences between these groups are small on level of education attained. Data from the 2005 American Community Survey shows that among working age PWDs, 34.5% had a high school diploma or equivalent and 28% had some college in contrast to people without disabilities, of which 27.9% had a high school diploma and 30.5% had some college. However, a greater percentage of people without disabilities had a bachelor's degree or more (30.1%) in comparison to PWDs (12.8%).[2]

There are no data comparing PWDs and people without disabilities on socialization and emotional coping skills or trainability/task flexibility, although employers express concerns in both areas.[3] However, two studies found employers generally held positive attitudes when asked about the social skills and personality traits of PWDs.[4]

Regarding dependability, the evidence is quite clear that PWDs fare well. Studies show that PWDs have equal or lower levels of absenteeism than people without disabilities, and that PWDs stay with jobs they occupy.[5] Employers surveyed in McFarlin et al. demonstrated positive attitudes toward turnover rates, absenteeism, and performance of workers with disabilities.[6]

Finally, there are no direct data comparing the motivation/satisfaction of PWDs and people without disabilities.

Nine studies conducted since 1987 all have reported positive attitudes on the parts of employers toward employees with disabilities that came from vocational rehabilitation or supported-employment programs.[7] This trend could be indicative of employers having much more confidence in hiring PWDs who have institutional evidence of an education that would teach the required KSAOs.

What can be concluded from this depiction of the KSAOs of PWDs? First, lower levels of education may inhibit the employability of individuals with disabilities for jobs requiring a bachelor's degree or higher. Employers will not hire individuals who do not have the necessary KSAOs to perform the job. Second, individuals with disabilities are equal to or better than individuals without disabilities on the criterion of dependability. That is, PWDs have average or better absenteeism and average or lower turnover than their nondisabled counterparts. Third, employers react favorably to demonstrated evidence of employees with disabilities possessing KSAOs, such as through a vocational or supported-employment work program. In other words, certification may improve employability by reducing employer uncertainty about the KSAOs of PWDs. Lastly, we simply don't know enough about how PWDs compare with people without disabilities across the criteria of socialization and emotional coping skills, trainability and task flexibility, and motivation/satisfaction.

EXPLANATION 2: PWDs HAVE LOWER JOB PERFORMANCE AND PRODUCTIVITY

Another explanation for the low employment rate of PWDs is that their job performance is lower and they are not as productive as employees without disabilities. Labor economists propose that in deciding on the types and amount of labor to use for producing a given level of output, firms will consider the contribution, or productivity of each input relative to its cost.[8] A firm's objective is to minimize its costs for a desired level of output. According to this perspective, employers will weigh the benefits versus the costs of hiring alternative applicants for a position. The costs of hiring include wages, nonwage compensation, training, and other investments, whereas the potential benefits include the value of employee productivity.

Employers may choose not to hire individuals with disabilities for the following reasons: (1) they believe individuals with disabilities are less productive than equally qualified individuals without disabilities, (2) they believe it will be more costly to hire individuals with disabilities because accommodations or other investments may be necessary to achieve the same level of productivity as people without disabilities, and (3) they believe individuals with disabilities will be heavy users of health care benefits, thus increasing the costs of providing those benefits to employees.

Evidence comparing the productivity of PWDs to people without disabilities is sparse. Greenwood and Johnson reviewed studies covering the period 1948 to 1981 and concluded that results support "a continuing record of quality performance."[9] Statistics from the U.S. Office of Vocational Rehabilitation show that 91% of workers with disabilities were rated either "average" or "better than average," the same as their counterparts without disabilities.[10] A study by Lee and Newman reported that 72% of employers who had hired persons with disabilities rated their job performance as average, above average, or excellent.[11] Employers surveyed in McFarlin et al. demonstrated positive attitudes toward turnover rates, absenteeism, and performance of workers with disabilities.[12] However, several studies show that employers who previously had not employed persons with disabilities had great concerns regarding productivity, proper job fit (i.e., having suitable menial or repetitive tasks for PWDs to perform), accidents or injuries on the job, and worker's compensation claims.[13]

As more jobs become knowledge work, utilizing computers and the Internet, it seems likely that productivity differences between PWDs and people without disabilities will become even more insignificant. As one individual with a disability describes, "Being a member of the e-generation, one can escape the bounds of a damaged body and compete on equal terms with those without disabilities."[14] Using the Internet, individuals with disabilities can communicate with colleagues, participate in meetings, and complete other work. Furthermore, working in cyberspace removes some of the stereotypes generated by face-to-face contact.

The information technology (IT) industry holds much promise for individuals with disabilities. "When someone is seated in front of a computer and communicating through a Web site, a wheelchair, a cane, or a hearing aide becomes invisible. That's why the IT field is such a nice fit for people with disabilities," says Richard Dodds, a 20-year veteran of IT and director of technology at Community Options, Inc., a national nonprofit group that provides employment and residential services for people with disabilities.[15] Thus, the Internet and computer technology become equalizers for PWDs—creating a level playing field.

In summary, the evidence shows no significant performance and productivity differences between PWDs and people without disabilities. However, there is still the perception that differences do exist between these two groups among employers, especially those employers who have not had experience with PWDs. Furthermore, as knowledge work and information technology become more ubiquitous in business and industry, differences in productivity between PWDs and people without disabilities should become less.

EXPLANATION 3: PWDs ENTAIL HIGHER COSTS THAN EMPLOYEES WITHOUT DISABILITIES

As a result of the passage of the Americans with Disabilities Act, many employers believe that costly accommodations and other investments are necessary in order to hire and maintain employees with disabilities and equalize productivity. A recent study found that the most common accommodations include special equipment (18%), scheduling of breaks or flextime (16%), task substitution (11%), office redesign (10%), computer software (10%), and increased access (10%).[16] While some accommodations may be costly, survey data collected by the Job Accommodation Network (JAN) for the President's Committee on Employment of People with Disabilities between October 1992 and July 1999 shows that among employers making accommodations, 71% of accommodations cost $500 or less, with 20% of those costing nothing.[17] Lengnick-Hall et al. found that 38% of human resource (HR) professionals indicated their organizations spent nothing on reasonable accommodations; 28% spent $1,000 or less; approximately 8% spent between $1,000 and $5,000; and approximately 14% spent more than $5,000.[18]

Other studies report accommodations that entail no cost number as high as 51–54%.[19] In addition, the annual amortized costs of these accommodations over their useful lifetime (or the tenure of PWDs employment) may be much lower.

Four studies found that employers were very concerned about perceived costs in accommodations for workers with disabilities.[20] Moreover, Hazer and Bedell found that a job applicant's request for accommodation can have a negative effect; the more disruptive the accommodation, the less suitable the person will be seen for hire.[21] One interesting viewpoint on the topic of accommodation costs was revealed in a focus group reported by Pitt-Catsouphes and Butterworth[22]: "Although several of the supervisors stated that they thought that most of the accommodations made at the workplace had not been particularly expensive, the financial burden often fell on the specific department where the employee with a disability was assigned. Given the firms' emphases on cost-cutting measures, many of the supervisors felt that this cost allocation system introduced disincentives to the hiring of individuals with disabilities."

In addition to job accommodation costs, researchers also have studied differences between PWDs and those without disabilities on costs related to lost time due to work injuries, accidents, and insurance costs. In general, findings show little or no differences between the groups on these cost criteria.[23]

In summary, accommodations for PWDs may entail additional costs to employers, but evidence to date suggests that these costs are usually minor and unlikely to tip the benefit-versus-cost assessment away from hiring this source of labor. However, there is support that shows those employers who are not aware of this evidence still have concerns regarding accommodation costs for employees with disabilities. Other costs, such as accidents, injury, and insurance, are not different between PWDs and those without disabilities.

EXPLANATION 4: EMPLOYERS FEAR LITIGATION ASSOCIATED WITH TERMINATING PWDs

One explanation that has been offered to account for the declining employment of PWDs during the 1990s after the passage of the Americans with Disabilities Act is that employers fear lawsuits related to hiring and firing them. A recent survey of HR professionals found support that this attitude is common.[24]

From July 1992 to September 1997 the Equal Employment Opportunity Commission (EEOC) received 90,803 charges under the Americans With Disabilities Act.[25] Of those charges filed directly with the EEOC, 29% were related to failure to provide accommodation, 9.4% were related to discrimination at the hiring stage, and 62.9% were for wrongful termination. Clearly, the largest percentage of charges concern claims of unfair termination. Thus, employers may fear that once hired, unsatisfactory employees with disabilities may be costly to terminate. However, statistics show this concern should not be an issue. Allbright and Lee reviewed a total of 696 lawsuits charging violations of the ADA.[26] Of these, 96% of the decisions were favorable for the employer, either through summary judgment or through merits of the case. Analysis of these cases suggests that if employers assess whether an individual is covered by law, and whether accommodation is reasonable, courts most often defer to the employer's judgment, resulting in minimal legal liability. Lee also goes on to posit that with the new Supreme Court ruling in 2002 regarding what constitutes a normal life act, the number of plaintiffs winning their cases will be less.

In summary, while the fear of litigation may have some impact on the employment of PWDs, evidence to date is indirect and inconclusive. However, employer concerns may be more overstated than justified.

EXPLANATION 5: EMPLOYERS DON'T HIRE PWDs BECAUSE OF COWORKER REACTIONS

Coworker reactions present a possibility for explaining why employers hire fewer workers with disabilities. Employers may fear that coworkers will react negatively to working with PWDs and thereby lower productivity, increase labor costs, and make their organizations less profitable. Greenwood and Johnson concluded that while the evidence for these concerns regarding PWDs is mixed, there is "a continuing concern about coworker relationships, particularly when mental and emotional disabilities are involved."[27]

What concerns might coworkers have about working with individuals with disabilities? Stone and Colella propose three possibilities.[28] First, coworkers may fear a negative effect on *work-related outcomes*. For example, individuals without disabilities may fear an increase in their workloads as a result of working with an individual with a disability. In conditions of task interdependence, coworkers may fear a loss of rewards if their own job performance is dependent on the performance of an individual with a disability. Colella et al. found some support for this reaction in a laboratory experiment.[29]

Second, coworkers may fear a negative effect on *personal outcomes*. Individuals without disabilities may fear that some disabilities are contagious (even when they are not). People without disabilities also may feel resentment regarding accommodations and special treatment received by PWDs.[30]

Third, coworkers may fear a negative effect on *interpersonal outcomes*. For example, coworkers may feel awkwardness, discomfort, ambivalence, and guilt about how they should interact with PWDs. This may result in avoidance behavior and exclusion of PWDs from formal and informal work groups. All of these coworker concerns may play an even more important role in organizations structured around teams, where team members get to hire their coworkers.

In summary, while there are plausible explanations for why coworkers may react negatively to employees with disabilities, there is virtually no empirical evidence to determine if these reactions are in fact commonplace.

EXPLANATION 6: EMPLOYERS DON'T HIRE PWDs BECAUSE OF CUSTOMER REACTIONS

Employers may fear that customers without disabilities may have negative reactions to interactions with employees with disabilities and transact less business with their organizations. Both explanations are plausible and, interestingly, both explanations were offered in the past to explain employer reluctance to hire other minority groups, such as women, Blacks, and Hispanics. However, this argument ignores the fact that PWDs earn $175 billion in discretionary income, which is almost two times the spending power of teens, and more than 17 times the spending power of tweens (those aged 8–12), two groups sought after by businesses.[31] By not hiring PWDs, organizations may be *losing* revenue as well.

While there is no research on this phenomenon, one might expect customers to have similar responses to those described previously for coworkers. For *work-related outcomes*, customers without disabilities may fear that employees with disabilities do not produce high quality products or are incapable of delivering the same level of service as workers without disabilities. For *personal outcomes*, customers without disabilities may hold similar fears as coworkers regarding the contagion of disabilities. *For interpersonal outcomes*, customers without disabilities may likewise fear feelings of awkwardness, discomfort, ambivalence, and guilt about how they should interact with PWDs. All of these explanations are plausible; however, there is no research that has been conducted in this area.

In summary, employers may choose not to hire individuals with disabilities because of fears about negative coworker and customer reactions (i.e., from coworkers and customers who do not have disabilities). Several theoretical explanations have been proposed that seem quite plausible. Unfortunately, virtually no research has been conducted to test the validity of these propositions.

CONCLUSION

In summary, we have found that first, PWDs are equivalent to nondisabled people in obtaining high school diplomas. However, a lower percentage of PWDs have bachelor's degrees or higher levels of education in contrast to people without disabilities. However, individuals with disabilities rate equal or better than people without disabilities on the criterion of dependability— lower absenteeism and turnover. We simply don't know enough about how PWDs compare to their nondisabled counterparts across other criteria that have been proposed.

Second, the evidence shows no job performance and productivity differences between PWDs and people without disabilities. Furthermore, as knowledge work and information technology become more ubiquitous in business and industry, differences in productivity between PWDs and people without disabilities should become less.

Third, accommodations for PWDs may entail additional costs to employers, but evidence to date suggests that these costs are usually minor and unlikely to tip the benefit-versus-cost assessment away from hiring this source of labor. Furthermore, there are no major differences between PWDs and employees without disabilities on accidents, workplace injuries, and insurance costs.

Fourth, while the fear of litigation may have some impact on the employment of PWDs, evidence to date is indirect and inconclusive. However, it appears that employer concerns may be overstated.

Fifth and sixth, while employers may choose not to hire individuals with disabilities because of fears about negative coworker and customer reactions (i.e., from coworkers and customers without disabilities), there is virtually no research to support these claims. However, several theoretical explanations have been proposed that seem quite plausible.

As this chapter has shown, most employer fears about hiring people with disabilities are not well founded. Unfortunately, many employers share these concerns and base their hiring decisions on inaccurate information. Consequently, people with disabilities don't get hired, employers miss out on valuable and talented employees, and society bears the costs of the unemployed.

SECTION TWO

Solutions: What Some Leading Companies Are Doing to Hire and Retain People with Disabilities

CHAPTER 3

Hewlett-Packard

Philip Gaunt

Hewlett-Packard (HP), located in Palo Alto, California, was founded in 1939 by Bill Hewlett and Dave Packard, both of whom were Stanford graduates. The company began life as a manufacturer of test and measurement instruments, and their first product was a precision audio oscillator. One of their earliest customers was Walt Disney Productions, which bought eight of their oscillators to test the Fantasound stereophonic sound system for the movie *Fantasia*. In 1968, HP came out with its 9100A desktop calculator, which is considered by many to be the first personal computer. As Bill Hewlett said at the time, "If we had called it a computer it would have been rejected by our customers' computer gurus because it did not look like an IBM."

The company later earned much respect for a variety of its products, including a number of handheld scientific and business calculators, oscilloscopes, logic analyzers, and other measurement instruments. In 1984, HP introduced inkjet and laser printers for the desktop, as well as a number of multifunction products, such as the single-unit printer/scanner/copier/fax machines. In the 1990s, HP expanded its computer product line, which initially had been targeted at university, research, and business customers, to reach private consumers. In 2002, HP merged with Compaq, a move intended to make the company a leader in personal computing. In 2004, the company reported revenues of almost $80 billion and a workforce of over 150,000 employees.

ACCESSIBLE PRODUCTS AND ACCESSIBLE JOBS

Former Chairman and CEO Carly Fiorina stated HP's position regarding accessibility: "From the beginning of our reinvention, we said that all our actions would be aimed at connecting people to the power of technology, harnessing it to lift human potential. In keeping that promise, HP made a commitment to provide leadership in designing accessible products and services for people with disabilities."[1] HP, which won the New Freedom Initiative Award for its stance with regard to people with disabilities (PWDs), strives to connect people to the power of technology and is working with local and global partners to build a foundation for universal access to basic technologies. The company focuses on making its products accessible to PWDs and partners with others to create and distribute assistive technologies. The company has an Accessibility Program Office that guides corporate-wide accessibility in product design, engineering, product development, marketing, Web, services, and support for PWDs. And it also employs people with disabilities in the development of accessibility guidelines, and in the design and testing of products and services. It was pointed out that there are some 49 million people with disabilities in the United States alone, and a huge number worldwide, and that is why "our products need to be accessible. We want folks to buy our products, and so there is a huge market. It is the business case that actually keeps it really moving forward. It is the business case that directs us in all the things that we do."[2]

When asked what motivated it to develop a proactive stance with regard to the employment and retention of people with disabilities (PWDs), HP responds that this stance grew out of a long-standing diversity department that was created some 25 years ago and which focused initially on affirmative action. So, it could be said that disability has always been part of the diversity picture. Over the years, specific units have been created to handle disability issues such as accessibility, training, and recruitment of PWDs. For example, within the Employee Relations Department there is a Management Disability Unit that helps employees who leave on short-term disability to work through the accommodation process when they return to work. This unit also works with persons who are not going out on disability but who still need an accommodation. All of these issues were formalized in a company-wide Accessibility Policy that was introduced in 2002.

TAKING DISABILITY EMPLOYMENT GLOBAL

Hewlett-Packard also demonstrates its commitment to PWDs globally. For example, the company maintains country action plans designed to promote and ensure inclusion of employees with disabilities. Recently, HP sponsored the European Year of People with Disabilities (EYPD) in 2003. This event promoted changes in hiring and employment laws to reduce discrimination and improve the employment of PWDs.

Being a global company, HP interacts with its own diversity directors in EMEA (Europe/Middle East/Africa) as well as AP (Asia Pacific). Diversity compliance has become a requirement in many European countries, as well as in Japan and China. It is probably going to be a requirement in other countries, too. Right now, it may be a requirement for government entities only, but in the future it is likely to affect businesses, too. One of the major initiatives undertaken by HP is the Disability Mentoring Day, which began as a national program, but which was held in 12 countries recently in about 25 sites. This initiative, sponsored by the American Association of People with Disabilities, resulted in the hiring of 13 persons in those 12 countries. Like some other proactive companies, HP has a corporate Leadership Council on Diversity, and its other companies all have their own diversity councils, although they are not specific to any one group. The HP Leadership Council is advisory to Sid Reel, who is Vice President of Global Inclusion and Diversity, and who formed the Council through HP's Executive Board. Again, speaking to the business case, Reel says, "We truly believe that diversity is a competitive advantage for us. We have seen that it contributes to our ability to attract new employees."[3]

MULTIPLE SOURCES FOR PWD RECRUITS

With regard to the recruitment of PWDs, top management has bought into the business case. Frontline supervisors, sometimes challenged with worker shortages, have been trained to expand their applicant pool, often going to a university they know and interacting with faculty to identify PWDs who also have the necessary technical skills needed for a particular position. They also work with recruiters having access to various labor pools. Some types of jobs, such as custodial staff, cafeteria staff, or gardeners, for example, are outsourced, but HP makes a point of working with employment agencies that are noted for their training of people with disabilities.

To increase the number of employees with disabilities in the company, Hewlett-Packard uses multiple sources. For example, they partner with several external organizations, including the American Association of People with Disabilities (AAPD), Career Opportunities for Students with Disabilities (COSD), the National Technical Institute for the Deaf and Hard of Hearing (NTID), the Business Leadership Network (BLN), the Department of Labor (DOL), and numerous rehabilitation and vocational centers throughout the United States.

Hewlett-Packard also recruits PWDs through schools, external network groups, and e-recruiting sources, such as Hiredisability.com and disabledperson.com. For example, in partnering with local schools, the company matches students with Hewlett-Packard employee mentors for a day (Hewlett-Packard is a sponsor of National Disability Employment Awareness Month and Disability Mentoring Day). They also have internships available to students for longer-term work experiences. One thing they stress at Hewlett-Packard is that they hire people who are qualified for the job—this applies to all of the employees with disabilities. They maintain their high standards for employment for all who are hired.

OVERCOMING COWORKER RESISTANCE

With regard to coworker resistance, Marleen Sloper, who oversees many diversity issues at HP, says that there can be awkwardness at first when a person with a disability is introduced into a unit. "I had a coworker who had no hearing, so our department learned sign language so that we could communicate a little. It was really good because it opened up the relations with this woman, who previously felt that she was isolated within the group."[4]

HP has a number of support groups for different disability categories, for example, physical, intellectual, and emotional. And it has a separate support group called the Disability Network, which is not specific to any particular disability. In fact, one does not have to have a disability to be part of it. Members may have a relative or know someone with a disability, so the purpose of the Disability Network is to educate, build awareness, and provide development.

Along these lines, there are a number of training programs on the company's intranet, which are open to all managers and employees. Many of these programs are general in nature, but more specific programs can be developed if they are requested. For example, the HP Accessibility Program, run by Michael Takemura, who is wheelchair bound and was largely responsible for the New Freedom Initiative Award, has set up a training program for HP's sales organization on product accessibility. Marleen Sloper has also set up her own site about the accommodation process. This is where managers can go if they hire a person with a disability or if an employee gets a disability, and are not sure what steps should be taken.

Bill Tipton, who is based in Cupertino, just a few miles south of Palo Alto, has been very closely involved with an employee resource group. Bill, a long-time employee of HP, lost his sight a few years ago and, after taking a year off, came back to work with the company and since then has worked very hard to help accommodate workers with disabilities—the visually impaired in particular. Bill explains that this resource group, which is not limited to PWDs, has proved to be very useful and supportive for those workers who do have disabilities. "We kind of just help each other and discuss challenges we might have and how we can work around some of these challenges. Our goal is to try to bring in speakers to help us learn, not necessarily things about disabilities, but also just how to be better professionals at work, just like any employees. We discuss those things as well as how to better do our jobs and pursue our career just like any other employee."[5]

When asked about HP's approach to the whole issue of hiring and retaining people with disabilities, he responds, "I do talk to a lot of disabled employees and so far all of them except one are still working, so they have been able to continue their jobs. They all run into problems. I talk to blind employees the most because I am blind and we run into the same kind of issues, but we are all still working and doing our jobs and that is a good thing."[6] With regard to assistive technology, Bill's group shares information about particular forms of assistive hardware with other individuals with other disabilities so they are more aware of what a specific person with a particular disability may need. As a member of the Technology Services Group, Bill and a number of other employees with disabilities are working on for-profit projects that help diversity both at HP as well as with external businesses, and this project provides information to diversity leaders at all levels all the way up to vice presidents, executives, and directors. "What I do within my project team is to try to leverage ways to get all the other employees within HP to know about these groups that exist today. We are going to do a video about diversity issues and employee resource groups and place it on a website."[7] Bill and his team also work out in the community. For example Bill sits on the boards of the Sensory Access Foundation and the Silicon Valley Council of the Plains, which is a local chapter of the national American Council of the Blind.

Regarding the issue of coworker reactions to PWDs, as well as the efforts being made by HP to accommodate them, Bill maintains that, "they are perfectly fine with them. There are no problems at all." On a more personal level, when prompted by Marleen Sloper, Bill talks of his own experience. "I haven't been blind my whole life," he says. "I became blind in May 1999 but when I returned back to the office I was with the same group I had left when I could see and could walk around the building. When I first came back I was in a wheelchair and my wife pushed me in and I met my group. Later on, when I actually did have mobility training and could walk around the building, it was kind of an odd feeling because people didn't know how to talk to me. They were very quiet, especially the people I knew beforehand. They were more quiet than complete strangers. I would go sit in the coffee room and complete strangers would come up and talk, but my regular coworkers, they were I guess used to seeing me when I had sight, and they had to get used to me walking around not being able to see. I guess they didn't want to overstep their boundary and help out where they might think that I didn't need help. If I had brought them into the room and explained it all to them right off it might have helped. So we just kind of went at it like we did but it worked out though."[8]

THE HP ACCESSIBILITY PROGRAM

Another key person interviewed is Michael Takemura, who is Director of the HP Accessibility Program. The chief responsibility of this program is to ensure that products and programs, and services and information for HP customers and partners, are accessible to people with disabilities and age-related impairments. Such programs could be for external uses—typically for customers—or they could be for internal uses such as training, or tools for engineers, web designers, or customer service agents. There is an overlap with Human Factors, but the main focus of the Accessibility Program is specific to the usability of and use of products for people with disabilities, and the compatibility and interoperability of HP projects with third-party assistive technology products that make up solutions for any customers.

With regard to age-related impairments, Michael points out that within the next five years or so, a majority of the population will be older than 45 years of age. It is critical then to look not only at products but also how customers procure them, how they use them, and how they refer to product documentation. All the way through the life cycle of the product we are looking to see how we can ensure that the product is accessible to people with disabilities or age-related impairments. In referring to customers, Michael explains that there are three primary market segments: the individual consumer, the small to medium business, and large corporate clients. There is also the public sector, which includes not only federal, state, and local government, but also education. The first segment is probably the strongest driver behind accessibility efforts, and there are now requirements in the United States as well as increasingly across Europe, Japan, New Zealand, and Australia that address regulation standards for the accessibility of information technology.

In the United States, there is Section 508 of the Rehabilitation Act that requires product accessibility, as well as to a certain extent Section 255 of the Telecommunications Act, although this has not been confirmed by case law. There are similar regulations in the U.K. and several European mandates with regard to design and accessibility for PWDs and the elderly, as well as in certain parts of Latin America. One interesting area right now, Michael observes, is the Middle East. This has a lot to do with war and the number of people becoming disabled in that region. In places like Saudi Arabia, even Israel, and the Middle East generally, there is a lot of activity in the area of assistive technology. Also, Section 508 is a significant driver in overseas markets. In fact, the primary issue that HP is working on in the IT industry is the formalization of such regulatory issues and standards worldwide so that there may be one single common standard as opposed to the fragmentation of multiple standards across regions or areas. As a result, activities occurring in one region certainly influence others and, in fact, recently, there were some people from Japan working with the U.S. government looking at how to set up legislation similar to the Americans with Disabilities Act (ADA) in Japan.

Internally, just as Bill Tipton's group works with employee resource groups related to disability, Michael Takemura's Accessibility Program also works "to educate, evangelize, help develop standards and processes, and bring them to different business units of different organizations within HP."[9] Another thing that Michael's program does is to hold an ongoing Global Accessibility Awareness Day, which is focused around workers with disabilities. Also, with regard to real estate, there is an organization whose sole purpose is to work on employee accommodations, including information technology accommodations and assistive technology, workspace, and all the other factors that go into the work environment. So, while they may not be directly involved with employees, in many cases, they are involved indirectly.

Michael Takemura's background originally was in account management and product marketing, but, given his spinal cord injury, which has made him into a wheelchair user, when Section 508 was coming in 1999 one of HP's vice presidents asked him to take a look at the 508 issue. Given his practical knowledge in the area of accessibility, he scoped out what the requirements of Section 508 were and developed a market plan for HP to meet these requirements. Also, given his previous positions, Michael had the skills to bridge engineering groups and marketing groups. He was able to explain to the engineers what some of the marketing influences and requirements were, and, conversely, he could take the work done by the engineers and give it a palatable format for consumers and users.

Another project overseen by Michael Takemura is Web-based training. In the past, most training was done face to face, but more recently a webinar approach was adopted and demand has grown considerably. The first project was for the sales and marketing department and this just focused on the basics because, as Michael says, "If you can imagine, there are people who have a difficult time grasping how people with disabilities may use our technology and make use of the tools we develop."[10] One example given was that of a sales person responding to a telephone call and saying, "Just give me the serial number of the product and we can help you. Then the caller says she cannot see the number and the sales person asks why not." "So, as a result we have developed training that goes over the basics of who our customers are with disabilities, how they use their technology, what are the market implications of legislation and the appropriate marketing requirements for a particular disability. Two other projects are specific to the Web development team to explain to them how persons with disabilities might interact with HP's Web presence, and how to make the Web presentation accessible. These have been used by customer support agents who get to talk to customers on the phone. Finally, an accessibility tool kit has been developed to deliver guidance and best practices to the engineering community to explain what are the requirements for designing accessible technology products like desktop notebooks, printers, scanners, cameras, fax machines, and pocket PCs."[11]

The perspectives provided by Tipton and Takemura are very personal, but they do speak to two key initiatives within HP: the employee resource groups and the accessibility program. HP's Sid Reel states that the increased global focus of its activities does not mean a radical departure from how the company has approached its diversity efforts, but it has meant an expansion of those efforts. She reports that HP now has some 50 employee resource groups and the number outside the U.S. has also grown considerably. The company funds the groups' efforts in conducting professional development activities and running communications-focused and networking events with other employees. "This has really helped increase morale."[12] The Accessibility Program guides corporate-wide accessibility for products designed for PWDs, who have become an increasingly important part of the company's consumer base. Meanwhile, internally, HP has introduced a broad array of accommodations for its employees. These include ergonomic office setups, special monitors or video devices, TTY telephones as part of the regular help-desk-supported office options, printers with audio signals, screen-reading software, alternate tagging of images on its website, two-way pagers for deaf employees, motorized carts for employees with mobility impairments, digital real-time captioning, and enhanced lumbar support in company vehicles.

SUMMARY

Like other flagship companies, Hewlett-Packard determined early on that it made sound business sense to fold disability into its overall diversity picture. This has served not only to increase its consumer base and sales but also to hire, train, and retain a labor pool that contributes in many different ways to the success of the organization.

The business case for hiring people with disabilities is closely coupled with the business case for designing products for people with disabilities—they represent a large and important labor and product market. Hewlett-Packard develops early pipelines to locate potential employees with disabilities, trains coworkers to feel comfortable with them and to communicate effectively with them, and provides affinity groups for social and professional support throughout their careers.

LESSONS LEARNED

From Hewlett-Packard's experience in hiring and retaining PWDs, the following lessons may be learned by other companies:

- Make hiring PWDs part of your overall diversity efforts.
- Make a business case for hiring PWDs.
- Use multiple sources for recruiting PWDs.
- Develop an early pipeline of PWD recruits through internships and partnerships with schools.
- Develop country action plans to ensure inclusion of PWDs at global locations.
- Train coworkers to feel comfortable working with PWDs.
- Train coworkers to communicate effectively with PWDs (e.g., sign language)
- For outsourced activities, use organizations known for training PWDs.
- Expand inclusion in affinity groups for people with disabilities to include friends and relatives.
- Include PWDs in the development of products and services for consumers with disabilities.

CHAPTER 4

Dow Chemical Company

Robert R. Hull

Dow Chemical Company, based in Midland, Michigan, is a Fortune 500 company with 2005 sales of $46.3 billion. Dow is a multinational company, doing business in more than 175 countries and employing more than 42,000 people, approximately 60% of them in North America.

In 2003, Dow won a citation from the American Society for Training and Development for its Employment Networks.[1] The focuses of these six diversity networks include African American employees; Asian Diversity; Disability Employees; Gays, Lesbians, and Allies; Hispanic Latin Employees; and the Women's Innovation Network. In the United States, Dow is a Gold Level member of the National Disability and Business Council, and participates in the Business Leadership Network.

Several factors appear to have inspired Dow's changes toward proactive diversity policies. First, there is a strong awareness of the demographic trends in the developed nations (North America, Europe, and Japan), which some have called an "impending crisis."[2] There simply are not enough educated and trained job seekers available to replace the large numbers of baby boomers (born 1943–1960) who will be retiring in the next decade.[3] This motivates a search for the best-qualified job candidates in previously untapped populations.

Second, legal requirements impact heavily on the makeup of the workforce. Quantitative data, in this case the composition of an employer's workforce, are used to define whether a company is employing persons from defined "underrepresented populations" within the United States. Specifically, Dow must demonstrate substantive efforts to meet or exceed the percentages of employees it hires/retains/advances into nine categories of jobs, from Officials/Managers to Service Workers, in order to compare favorably to industry-wide data reported for Sector Industrial Code 281: Industrial Inorganic Chemicals, as used by the Equal Employment Opportunity Commission (EEO, 2001).[4] Racial/Ethnic groups considered to be "underrepresented" include Black, Hispanic, Asian American, and American Indian. In addition, the male-female balance in the nine occupational categories is compared between the company and its industry.

The response at Dow is to emphasize appropriate training. "We are trying real hard to educate our recruiters that underrepresentation is another factor or facet of the selection process. We aren't going to minimize the right educational requirements or experience or knowledge and skills to satisfy a quota, but underrepresentation must come into play when you are implementing a good selection process. In fact, I often hear discussion going the other way: we <u>must</u> consider a diverse candidate or one with disabilities for fear of people thinking we are not an inclusive employer."[5]

IDENTIFY THE MOST STRINGENT WORLD STANDARDS

Note that disability is not an "underrepresented" category for EEO review in the United States. This is not the case, however, for some other countries where Dow does business. Germany, Italy, Spain, Brazil, and Japan, among others, have legal quotas (usually 5% of the company's workforce) requiring the employment of persons with disabilities. In many countries, a company that does not meet its quota can alternatively make a contribution to a nonprofit organization ("pay a fine") that helps persons with disabilities find employment.[6] A key element of Dow's proactive human resource policy stance is that whatever is the most stringent requirement worldwide is then established as the standard or goal for the company. Dow even advertises on its website for a career option of Strategic Center Specialist, part of whose function is to "Identify global industry best practices and integrate them into the company."[7] Reaching such policy standards allows Dow to be nimble, and to move rapidly as business opportunities arise, without being delayed by last-minute efforts to meet labor requirements.[8] Such a policy has a further efficiency payoff: "No way can I keep track of the uniqueness of living and working and managing workforces in each of the countries where we are, so we look for the country that has the highest standards and that becomes our global standard."[9]

BENCHMARK PRACTICES

Benchmarking practices and other quantitative approaches to issues are a very strong emphasis at Dow. "O.K., we are a company of engineers so we are pretty anal about our statistics."[10] Each Employment Network aligns to the Diversity and Inclusion Group, with some networks being quite global and others quite local.[11] The Diversity Network has about 100 participants on their [email] distribution list globally. "We have made the transfer from being a company that has different plants outside the U.S. to a company that is U.S. based but doing business internationally to a truly global company. When we work at the whole diversity effort and we think about *what we can manage, what we can track*, our CEO's vision for us is that we deliver a workforce that reflects the place where we live and work."[12]

Disability, of course, is notoriously difficult to track, as there are legal protections in almost every country against requiring people with disabilities to disclose them. Dow, as an award-winning Six Sigma company, finds the absence of disability identifiers to be particularly difficult.[13] The Dow Diversity and Inclusion Group is making a proactive attempt to overcome this difficulty. In 2005 they launched a two-phase global project to gather information from former employees who left the company voluntarily within the past three years.

First, they created a database of all relevant pieces of information from their archived human resource files. They then mined this data to discover quantitative patterns that were correlated with the decision to leave. (Among these predictors, interestingly, was the employee's geographic driving distance to work.)[14] Second, they conducted face-to-face interviews with the former employees ("What did you like about Dow?" "What caused you to leave?"), and had them complete a written survey designed to validate the face-to-face interview. As former employees, interviewees could be asked legally if they are a person with a disability, and they could voluntarily choose whether or not to respond. Furthermore, the responses to the interviews and written surveys could be segmented by the six categories represented by the Employment Networks. In this way, the human resources group could look differentially at its policies and their impact on employees with disabilities, as part of the diversity picture.

CREATE EMPLOYEE NETWORKS

Creation of the six Employment Networks appears to be key among the changes made. The group with the greatest longevity, the Women's

Innovation Network, was created in 1985 when the then CEO asked a group of women employees to form a "Women's Issue Committee" to help the executive team identify the barriers to more women joining the company. "This was a real pivotal point."[15] Kathy McDonald, Director of the Global Diversity and Inclusion Group, indicated she had been invited to serve on this group even "as a baby in my career. My mentor was an engineer who was blind as the result of an industrial accident at Dow."[16]

An interviewer asked, "Why does Dow now have six, and not more or fewer, Employment Networks?" The response was that "these six employee groups have come forward and made their business case for formal support as an Employment Network. Each Network has an Office of Chief Executive sponsor and they are all required to have two senior level coaches as active participants. They have a Charter, they have an annual Action Plan that gets reviewed and approved, they have an [intranet] website, etc. Each year the Networks come before the Global Diversity and Inclusion Group and make the business case for their budget. Do they want to make outside donations, do they want to provide scholarships at universities, do they want to conduct internal education—these are sample plans. They are very employee-driven, and what we get from them is help in setting strategies and employee research. We often speak with them about 'an environment free from barriers to productivity.' These are the groups that have emerged so far."[17]

The Employment Networks do not appear to play as much of a consumer-reference group role as would the Affinity Groups at other companies, for example, as Dow is not primarily a retail company. The bulk of its sales are business-to-business, providing chemical compounds for other manufacturing processes. The Dow networks have a more limited human resource–oriented role, rather than responding to the initiatives of other departments such as marketing, sales, or accessible technology as at Microsoft. They often serve as research focus groups on diversity issues, as will be seen later.

ALIGN WORKFORCE LEADERSHIP WITH COMPANY POLICIES

Dow makes proactive efforts to align its workforce leadership with the company policies. They provide a two-day classroom workshop on "Understanding Diversity and Inclusion" that includes a four-hour teleconference exercise involving highly diverse work teams from around the globe. "This teleconference gets the highest satisfaction markings in terms of value added and quality content of any of the sessions that we offer."[18]

Like other large companies, Dow did at the time (1990) and continues now to conduct extensive training in the United States on the Americans with Disabilities Act (ADA). Globally, they have implemented a three-hour training course on their company code of conduct, "The 13 Global People Policies," which includes employee harassment and discrimination policies, and made it mandatory for their 4,700 global people managers.[19]

DIG DEEPER TO UNCOVER BARRIERS TO PEOPLE WITH DISABILITIES

As time has moved on since 1990 and the ADA, the company has tried to look deeper into their policies and practices, beyond the legal requirements. The Six Sigma methodology that permeates the company is evident here as well. "For example, we are looking at our current recognition programs in two ways. First, we are looking at the entire past utilization data for the awards: who received them. The data is what it is and I didn't create it and you didn't create it, but there is something here, however, that is telling us that we may be at risk." Then comes the Six Sigma technique of root cause analysis: "Second, we are looking at the content of the program to say, for example, 'Is there an unconscious bias such that employees that work virtually, which a number of our employees with disabilities do, might be excluded because they are less visible to us (in the hallways, at the water cooler, etc.)?' Then we are looking to see if there are steps in the process of how we implemented the recognition event itself that might reflect unconscious bias."[20] Dow is perhaps relatively unique in the degree to which they use a business methodology such as Six Sigma to pursue their diversity agenda.

THE BENEFITS OF CHANGE

When asked the standard question about any lessened turnover or absenteeism benefits to the company from employing persons with disabilities, the answer was intriguing and somewhat novel. "If my senses are correct, employees with disabilities have a lower turnover rate but absenteeism is about what it is for all employees and it may be just a slight bit higher. Employees with disabilities tend to experience their sick days bunched together owing to a more intensive episode of their disability, rather than having them scattered throughout the year. This may be somewhat more difficult for a manager."[21]

An additional benefit of the change toward diversity and inclusion is Dow's public face—its branding. Dow's website gives further evidence of the company's transformation from a national to an international to a global company. The website repeatedly makes a business case for its global diversity and inclusion focus.[22]

- "Dow is in the advantageous position of having a multitude of backgrounds, languages, cultures, nationalities, work styles, personal experiences, and mindsets to tap into. Embracing the unique differences of its employees gives Dow the ability to generate unique solutions for customers and operate successfully in any culture or location"

- "To be successful in this more global marketplace, Dow must accept and embrace diversity. At the most basic level, that means having a balanced employee population in terms of nationality, gender, and race. But equally important is our ability to accept differences in thought, style, manner, and experience. To achieve our goals for performance and growth, we must leverage the creativity and talents of all our people. And our global diversity strategy will help get us there"

- "What is diversity at Dow? Dow has a simple definition: Diversity is difference. We recognize, value, and leverage our differences for competitive advantage. The concept of difference is universal. It can be understood and interpreted in the context of each individual culture"

- "The bottom line is that we are serious about providing opportunities for all employees to flourish regardless of what makes them different. After all, innovation doesn't come from being just like everyone else"

SUMMARY

Once again, achieving the vision for diversity at Dow is a highly quantitative process. "Each of Dow's four [Diversity] Vision elements will be tested against benchmarking data, specific business and functional goals, surveys, audits, and reports from our databases. This measurement will help the company know how it is doing on the diversity journey, and guide our future activities."[23]

While disability as a category is "fuzzy" (because of issues of non–self-disclosure and confidentiality) so also are other categories used by human resource managers: gender (male, female, transgendered?) and race (are two employees, one born in New Mexico of formerly Mexican parents and one born in Paraguay of German-speaking parents both "Hispanic"?). It nevertheless is a testimony to the vision of diversity and inclusion at Dow Chemical Company that it seeks novel ways—such as interviewing former employees—to assess as accurately as possible whether it is being proactive with its employees with disabilities.

LESSONS LEARNED

- Take a global perspective on hiring people with disabilities (PWDs).
- Provide employee networks/affinity groups with a budget. Assign a senior executive to sponsor the group.
- Use employee networks/affinity groups as a research laboratory. Observe these groups to learn how to improve HR practices and policies affecting PWDs.
- Use quantitative and qualitative data to evaluate the impact of HR practices and policies on PWDs. Test for biases or unintentional consequences of policies and adjust accordingly.

CHAPTER 5

SunTrust Banks

Nancy Bereman and Stephanie J. Hargrave

SunTrust Banks Inc. is based in Atlanta, Georgia, and is one of the nation's largest commercial banking operations, with total assets in 2006 of $178.9 billion. It operates 1,677 retail branches in Alabama, Arkansas, Florida, Georgia, Maryland, Mississippi, North Carolina, South Carolina, Tennessee, Virginia, West Virginia, and the District of Columbia. The Bank has approximately 34,000 employees as of March 2006.[1]

SunTrust has what they call a Corporate Commitment Program for PWDs. This is a company-wide initiative that includes *internal* elements (efforts to improve accessibility for employees and customers) and *external* elements (efforts to share knowledge and encourage other employers to increase hiring of people with disabilities [PWDs]). They support these efforts by allocating staff, funding, and resources.

A BOTTOM-UP APPROACH

SunTrust Banks Inc. has developed a multipronged program to enhance their employment of PWDs. The focus on hiring PWDs began with one customer service representative in a bank branch who was able to communicate with sign language.[2] Customers with disabilities recognized this skill as an asset to their relationship with the bank. Soon thereafter, more customers with hearing disabilities began to frequent the branch. This single employee identified an opportunity to expand the services of the bank to customers with hearing disabilities and brought this opportunity to the attention of the management team. This led to the provision of additional services for customers with other types of disabilities. As a result, this bottom-up approach—coming from the field office—provided compelling justification for hiring PWDs throughout the company.

Soon, this proactive stance with customer service translated into hiring practices within the bank's Human Resources department. Katherine McCary stated that SunTrust and the banks that have been merged with the SunTrust organization have been "hiring people with disabilities and retaining people with disabilities but . . . didn't think of it as a proactive activity."[3] In the early 1990s, the banking industry found that the pool of candidates for all positions was limited. As a consequence, banks such as SunTrust reached out to minorities and women. Included in this outreach to different populations were PWDs.

Initially, disability etiquette training was developed and provided to recruiters and staffing managers in order to prevent any misunderstandings that could occur if the management employees are not aware of the laws and situations associated with hiring PWDs. One large phone campaign required approximately 600 temporary employees, and several PWDs were hired, owing to the proactive stance of the hiring manager for the project. When that project proved successful, other managers in the bank wanted to know her "secret," and she was identified as an internal champion for the hiring of PWDs. This bottom-up approach to promoting the hiring and retention of PWDs has proven effective in reducing resistance to change throughout the company.

REACHING OUT TO OTHER BUSINESSES

This initial campaign led to the self-nomination and selection of SunTrust for the SHRM National HR Innovative Practice Award.[4] This award provided the recognition necessary to take the lead in the development of a business-to-business educational opportunity to teach others about the successes of SunTrust in hiring PWDs. SunTrust became the lead employer in the establishment of the Virginia Business Leadership Network. The Business Leadership Network (BLN) was categorized under the President's Committee for the Employment of People with Disabilities in the late 1990s, and seemed the appropriate place to begin such an initiative into hiring practices for diversity throughout the region served by the bank.

After the development of the Virginia BLN, SunTrust became an active leader in Business Leadership Networks in Virginia, Florida, Tennessee, Maryland, and the District of Columbia. The programs developed and shared through these partnerships have resulted in the "successful employment and retention of more than 160 individuals with disabilities."[5] SunTrust has gone on to become active in the creation of the United States Business Leadership Network (USBLN), and in the development of a national volunteer organization designed "to educate employers about hiring and marketing their job opportunities to people with disabilities." The bank even supplied Katherine McCary (Director of SunTrust's Disability Resource Center) to serve as the chairperson for the USBLN. In this role, she has helped the organization achieve nonprofit status, establish chapter guidelines, develop an accessible website, and create bylaws.

In addition, the bank initiated the Assistive Technology Loan Fund Authority in Virginia to aid in the provision of "favorable loan terms and finance rates for people with disabilities, as well as for employers who hire and advance people with disabilities."[6] The bank is a partner in programs in Florida, Maryland, and Virginia to provide loans to PWDs to aid in the purchase of assistive technology, building improvements, and other aids in increasing access to the business or residence of those who apply.

EXPANDING PROGRAMS INTERNALLY

SunTrust has developed an intranet site entitled Accessing Community Talent (ACT) which is "designed to encourage managers to attract non-traditional qualified applicants who are not typically recruited by corporate human resource departments."[7] They also participate in a minority procurement program for vendors and suppliers—one component of which emphasizes using businesses owned and operated by PWDs.

SunTrust has developed in-house programs to aid in making their workforce as representative of their customer base as possible. These programs include development of Diversity Councils across the SunTrust network, which enable members of different populations of diversity to participate in the Business Leadership Networks and the development of efforts within the network to optimize the hiring and retention of persons from these populations.

The Diversity Councils have a top-down structure, from executive-level employees through subcommittees of employees tapped for participation who have responsibility for different regional activities. The Disability Mentoring Day—held in each region—is an example of the Disability Diversity Council projects. This project helps develop a pipeline of potential talent for future employment from members of that diversity group. Disability Mentoring Day has been expanded to include a developing relationship with Career Services and The Career Opportunities for Students with Disabilities (COSD) through the University of Tennessee. Through this relationship, SunTrust has developed the Emerging Leader's Program that targets high achieving college students with disabilities into summer internships and the potential for future employment within the network.[8]

SunTrust has taken the lead as a national sponsor of National Disability Mentoring Day, and hosted 183 youth with disabilities in 2003. The leadership of SunTrust has also volunteered to operate a pilot program to expand the Workforce Recruitment Program of the United States Department of Labor and ODEP, which will provide another source of valuable talent for the human resources of SunTrust.[9]

THE DISABILITY RESOURCE CENTER

Once employees with disabilities were hired and retained within the Sun-Trust network, the bank developed the Disability Resource Center to identify and meet the needs of the growing population of employees with disabilities within the workforce. This Disability Resource Center is responsible for accommodations and access to assistive technology that may be required by employees with disabilities, as well as the development of retention and advancement strategies for those employees. As with many of the employers awarded the New Freedom Initiative Award, SunTrust Banks Inc. has centralized its budget for accommodations as well as centralized its sponsoring of internships and mentoring activities through the Disability Councils.

One challenge SunTrust identified was the advancement of employees with disabilities. Medicare and Medicaid regulations place restrictions on the amount of money that many PWDs may earn in order to retain their benefits. These rules have limited the promotion of some employees with disabilities, because with promotion often comes longer hours and increased pay. Sun-Trust has also been proactive in meeting this challenge, developing an Employer Tool Kit. This is a Web-based tool that helps educate managers on how PWDs can gain employment without losing the benefits these employees need. The Tool Kit is available not only within SunTrust, but also to the United States Business Leadership Network members.[10]

CUSTOMERS WITH DISABILITIES

Targeting PWDs in recruitment and learning about their special needs has helped Sun Trust develop products and services that are accessible to customers with disabilities. As CEO Humann says, "SunTrust is committed to including and retaining individuals with disabilities in our workforce and serving customers in our marketplace. One very positive outgrowth of the recruitment and retention activity is that we learn from our employees about their needs and are able to develop products and services that are friendlier to customers with disabilities." For example, over 30 customers with disabilities requested and received bank statements in Braille, large print, or audiotape. Other customers received services provided by sign language interpreters. Consequently, part of Sun Trust's success can be attributed to linking their efforts to hire and retain PWDs directly to the bottom line: better employees and increased customer satisfaction and retention.

SUMMARY

When asked if the federal tax breaks, such as the Work Opportunity Tax Credit, were incentives to hiring individuals with disabilities, Katherine Mc-Cary identified that these tax credits are often cumbersome and difficult to manage, and that any gains that SunTrust may obtain through them are not enough to motivate these changes. Instead, she suggests, these changes were internally motivated, based on the need for qualified employees from all walks of life.[11]

SunTrust Banks Inc. identified a need in their customers that sparked a company-wide shift in culture toward hiring PWDs. When the business case was made—which identified the success of the programs that emphasized hiring PWDs—the company expanded its search for this often overlooked talent and developed a pipeline for the identification of future employees with disabilities. The success mushroomed into a need to share this innovative programming with other community business leaders, and led to better understanding of this group of potential employees. SunTrust has spent a great deal of manpower and developed innovative programs and tools to make the hiring of PWDs desirable in their own network, as well as to other businesses through the National Business Leadership organizations they lead.

LESSONS LEARNED

From SunTrust Banks' experience in hiring and retaining PWDs, the following lessons may be learned by other companies:

- Don't just provide lip service to your commitment to hiring PWDs. Allocate staff, funding, and resources to demonstrate your support.

- Provide a centralized disability resource center to distribute information and develop programs regarding PWDs. Consult with managers and units on how best to integrate PWDs in the workplace.

- Top managers must emphasize the business case for diversity.

- Assign top managers to diversity initiatives and report progress and accomplishments.

- Align diversity initiatives with business strategy.

- Take a bottom-up approach to demonstrating why hiring PWDs is beneficial to the organization. Demonstrate how hiring PWDs can solve problems in the field offices.

- Link the hiring of PWDs to customers and the bottom line. Use the opportunity for learning about employees with disabilities to learn about customers with disabilities.

- Proactively recruit PWDs before they enter the labor market. Use mentoring and internship programs to identify talented PWDs.

- Train recruiters on how to interview PWDs.

- Provide a centralized budget for reasonable accommodations.

- Focus on accessibility not just for employees, but for customers, too.

- Use multiple communication venues to emphasize the importance of hiring PWDs.

- Provide sponsorship for events promoting PWDs outside of the company.

- Use vendors and suppliers owned and operated by PWDs when possible.

- Use a combination of top-down and bottom-up approaches to promote hiring and retaining PWDs.

CHAPTER 6
A&F Wood Products

Philip Gaunt

A&F Wood Products, located in rural Howell, Michigan, is owned and operated by brothers Jason, Steven, and Patrick Korte, as well as their two sisters, Donna and Judy. The company, founded in 1965 by their father Aloysius Korte and his brother Frank, manufactures wooden doors and pocket door frames, which are now distributed nationwide.

When the brothers took over the company in 1991 they wanted to expand the distribution of their products from Michigan and three surrounding states to a much larger market. This meant increasing productivity while keeping material costs down. It also meant forming a national sales staff and developing new marketing strategies, which they have since done. Its current workforce of 20 now includes 7 persons with disabilities and the company is looking to hire more.

TAKING A CHANCE ON PEOPLE WITH DISABILITIES

As the company began to expand, it found itself very short of people and was having a difficult time recruiting suitable employees despite repeated attempts working with employment agencies and other local sources. Then one day, as the brothers tell the story, a social worker approached them and recommended someone who happened to have a disability. They interviewed the person in question and soon saw that it was not going to work out. The social worker then recommended another person with a disability. This time the interview was very positive, the person was hired and still works for the company, where he is

NO LIMITS ON JOBS THEY CAN DO

Needless to say, the company has been obligated to make workplace accommodations for most of the jobs performed by workers with disabilities. In some cases this has involved the use of a job coach as well as making software and telephone systems more accessible, particularly to one blind worker, BB, who works part-time in the office but who also runs an aluminum punching machine and often has to use a staple gun. In the office, the telephone system has been fitted with specific rings so that BB knows which phone is ringing and on which line. Adapting the aluminum punching machine was another matter, but BB was determined to succeed. So, the factory foreman, who is amazingly supportive of his workers with disabilities, went to the machine, closed his eyes, and spent hours studying and mapping out movements that would enable BB to do the job with complete safety, which is a major concern for management. She now runs the machine very successfully and, according to management, does a better job of counting and packing finished products than some previous unimpaired workers.

Another anecdote, which speaks to the wonderfully supportive culture that has developed at A&F, is the fact that BB is willing to try anything. There are forklift trucks that run around the factory floor all day and that of course could be dangerous to a blind person moving from a work station to the break room, office, or restrooms. So BB was told to be extremely careful, as were the drivers. One day, during a break, one of the brothers told BB to climb up on a forklift, showed her the controls and let her drive it down a broad avenue in the factory, shouting out instructions as she went. She was elated and the whole workforce cheered as she climbed down. Throughout the day, there is always someone willing to guide her to and from her workstations and the break room.

PARTNERING WITH LOCAL AGENCIES

The company works closely with vocational rehabilitation and Work Skills Corporation to train workers with disabilities. One very successful example is a hearing-impaired worker who needed communication and computer skills in order to do his work effectively, which is running a giant wood saw. As one of the brothers explains, one problem with running a large wood saw is that the operator needs to know when a blade is becoming dull and likely to break down. After working in the wood industry for many years, operators can tell just by the sound whether a blade is about to go down. How would this work for someone who is hearing impaired? It turned out that, with a little training, the deaf operator was able to tell just from the vibrations. Working closely with one of the brothers, this worker is now successfully turning out pre-hung units on the kinds of doors that are sold in large quantities at stores such as Home Depot or Lowe's.

The first worker with a disability to be hired by A&F works four days a week punching aluminum track. DD's workstation was modified to eliminate foot pedal punching to make it more user friendly. This worker, DD, has been instrumental in welcoming newer workers with disabilities and in helping build the very special culture that makes A&F such a great place to work for persons with disabilities. When asked about how members of the public react to their workers with disabilities, the brothers point out that theirs is a wholesale business and there is little contact with retail customers. However, they say that DD is a great public relations guy for the company. When a truck driver or delivery person walks into the factory, DD is always the one to show them where they need to go and will often walk them excitedly to the office. The drivers are a little surprised by DD's excitability and manner, but he is patently such a good man that there has never been a negative comment.

SUMMARY

Obviously, given its size and line of work, A&F Wood Products is very different from the other companies studied in this book. But, that said, there are some common features, too. The first is that it is convinced that it makes business sense to employ persons with disabilities. In the case of A&F, given a serious labor shortage in the mid-1990s, it could not have expanded its business as well as it has without the abilities and hardworking attitudes of its workers with disabilities. Having experienced the skills of its first worker with a disability, A&F developed a policy of hiring more workers with disabilities. Another finding shared by other businesses is that workers with disabilities tend to be more loyal and to stay with the company that employs them. This reduces the cost or hiring and training new workers, which can be a substantial saving. A&F, like other businesses, has accepted the cost and desirability of workplace accommodations, not only because they are needed but because they can also improve productivity. Like many of its larger counterparts, A&F has adopted management policies that have built a truly supportive culture for its workers with disabilities. Finally, A&F has become a strong champion of workers with disabilities and has learned to work closely with local rehabilitation and training and counseling organizations. "We don't go out and brag about it," says one of the brothers, "but when you talk to others and tell them if you want to find a great working force, here is what you have to try, because it has been wonderful for us, the reaction is, 'Where do I go and how do I start out?'"

As the New Freedom Initiative Award presented to the company states, "A&F Wood Products shows its commitment to a diverse workforce, including people with disabilities, by using assistive technology, partnering with organizations that have expertise in identifying potential job barriers, and providing a diversified training program."

LESSONS LEARNED

From A&F Wood Products' experience in hiring and retaining people with disabilities (PWDs), the following lessons can be learned by other companies:

- Small businesses do not need formal human resource programs to hire PWDs. They just need to think creatively.
- Use early successes in hiring PWDs to lower obstacles and encourage receptivity.
- Embrace a philosophy of "ability not disability."
- Do not limit the jobs available to PWDs on the basis of preconceived stereotypes.
- Provide a supportive environment for PWDs. Be willing to go beyond the standard employer-employee relationship.
- Adapt work schedules to public transportation schedules for PWDs who use public transportation.
- Take advantage of tax incentives for hiring PWDs.

CHAPTER 7

Giant Eagle Inc.

Nancy Bereman and Stephanie J. Hargrave

Giant Eagle Inc. is a privately owned retail grocery chain based in Pittsburgh, Pennsylvania. The grocery chain operates over 200 stores in four states (Ohio, Pennsylvania, Maryland, and West Virginia) and employs over 35,000 workers, making them one of the market leaders in the region they serve.[1] Founded in 1918, Giant Eagle has been promoting successful innovations for customers consistently for nearly 100 years. Included in these innovations in the last decade are the introductions of Cookie Cards, which accumulate points for purchases with the proceeds benefiting local children's hospitals, and the Eagle's Nest childcare and activity center for shoppers' children. The company's mission statement reflects their community focus, stating, "We will provide service and products that meet or exceed our customers' requirements at all times. To do this, every employee must fully understand our customers' needs and the requirements of their jobs and meet them every time. We will measure our success by the satisfaction of our customers."[2]

Giant Eagle Inc. has been successful in the hiring and retention of over 315 employees with disabilities. Of these employees, approximately 56 have been employed with the company between 10 and 34 years, and about 79 have been employed between 5 and 9 years.[3]

Speaking for the company, Dale Giovengo identified that the employment of persons with disabilities came from personal experience with members of the community and employees, rather than a formal, business case. "It seem(ed) like everybody (they) talked to had somebody in their family that had a disability or some had contact or . . . experience with somebody with a disability."[4] This, in addition to the necessity of finding good workers who had the skills to do the job and would have relatively lower turnover rates, caused the company to redirect its focus to the development of a training program for the workers with disabilities in their communities.

PROJECT OPPORTUNITY

Beginning in the 1980s, the ownership and corporate leaders had created a climate that was open to new ideas—including the training and hiring of persons with disabilities. The local association for the blind in Pittsburgh identified this openness and proposed a program to provide clients as employees and job coaches to aid in their success at the jobs available. This was a new idea at the time and Giant Eagle accepted the proposal. As Giovengo stated, "it kind of mushroomed" from there.[5]

Project Opportunity—a school-to-work program for persons with disabilities—was developed in 1991. Using the training and job coaching model that was originally proposed by the association for the blind, Giant Eagle's Project Opportunity was designed to "give students with disabilities (ages 16–21) realistic employment targets, independence, self-confidence, and ultimately a permanent job with Giant Eagle."[6]

Project Opportunity partners with vocational rehabilitation centers, public schools, and community groups that champion persons with disabilities, such as cerebral palsy and low vision, to identify potential employees for their three phased training program.

PHASE I

Project Opportunity is a three-phased program. The first phase of the Project Opportunity program is educational. Specifically, students are paired with a teacher who works with them for 20 days on job readiness skills. These skills include appearance, attendance, and attitudinal issues that the student may not have encountered previously. They are taught such things as the importance of doing well in class, what to wear to a job interview, and proper behavior on the job. At the same time, Giant Eagle representatives train the teachers at their stores in the tasks and details of the jobs that the students may be assigned to in the following weeks.[7] This ensures that the teachers are instructing the students properly by training them for success in particular jobs. This initial phase also serves to identify those students who may not be a good fit for the Giant Eagle opportunity.

Phase II

In the second phase, the trained students are placed at a centrally located Giant Eagle Store and these students work in selected departments for a period of three to four weeks (Monday through Friday; 9:00 AM—1:00 PM). During this time, teachers as well as job mentors from Giant Eagle work to help the students learn the specific details of the jobs they are assigned. At the end of the trial placement at the centrally located store, students are evaluated. If the skills have been developed for success, the student is then assigned to a similar position at a local Giant Eagle store.

Phase III

The third and final phase is the continued work at this local store for the duration of the 45-day probationary period required of all Giant Eagle employees—with the aid of a job coach to answer questions and solve problems. These placements have the potential to become permanent for the trainees. Should the job coach identify problems with the employee, Giant Eagle management works to provide retraining or reassignment in order to optimize the employee's performance.[8]

A specific challenge for Giant Eagle is the negotiations with union representatives regarding the jobs and performances of its members. Because of the unique situations posed by some of the employees with disabilities, flexibility in union contract provisions must be negotiated. Giovengo identified a particular situation where an employee with a disability required a transfer to a different department, due to difficulty in the existing work environment. Traditionally, the union rules would prohibit such a move, but negotiation for the situation allowed the transfer to occur without incident.[9]

DISABILITY AWARENESS TRAINING

Every two years, Giant Eagle conducts an extensive Disability Awareness Training for their human resource managers. This training consists of a review of the Americans with Disabilities Act (ADA), interviewing skills for hiring people with disabilities (PWDs), and disability simulations. Held offsite at a YMCA camp, Giant Eagle invites various agencies, such as the Office of Vocational Rehabilitation, Pittsburgh Vision Services, the Pittsburgh School for the Deaf, and the Epilepsy Foundation to participate. Half of the day is spent learning about the ADA and interviewing skills, while the remaining half of the day the human resource managers spend actually experiencing disabilities. Stations are manned by job coaches who simulate for the human resource managers what it is like for someone with a disability. For example, a wheelchair exercise allows the human resource managers to perform everyday activities, such as using a drinking fountain, maneuvering through doors and up and down ramps, and reaching for something on a shelf.

This not only alleviates some of the negative misperceptions and attitudinal barriers toward persons with disabilities from the employees in each store, but provides the human resources manager with contacts to leaders in these organizations to identify potential employees and to ask for help if questions arise regarding clients who become employees. Giovengo identified that, despite some initial negative reactions by employees or customers to working or interacting with persons with disabilities in the stores, the overwhelming majority of the reactions have been positive.[10]

A COMMITMENT TO ACCOMMODATIONS

Giant Eagle has a strong commitment to providing opportunities for PWDs, which has its roots in their people philosophy:

- Each individual will receive thorough training for the job responsibility they are assigned.
- Each individual will have defined responsibilities and the means to accomplish the tasks assigned him or her.
- Each individual's needs and wants will be met whenever possible.
- Each individual will be treated fairly.

The company enacts this philosophy for PWDs by providing no limits on what jobs they may perform. For example, PWDs hold the gamut of jobs at the stores: baker, bakery counter clerk, customer service clerk, florist, deli clerk, stock clerk, prepared foods clerk, cashier, maintenance, lot attendant, meat cutter, meat wrapper, video clerk, produce clerk, stock clerk, point of sales clerk, playroom attendant, office clerk, and human resource manager. Furthermore, Giant Eagle accommodates people with a wide range of disabilities: deafness, hearing impairment, blindness, vision impairment, mental retardation, emotional disability, learning disability, cerebral palsy, autism, epilepsy, spina bifida, and paraplegia.

Accommodations for PWDs start with the hiring process. Giant Eagle uses an automated hiring system, but it has accommodations for PWDs with vision and hearing impairments. In addition, once hired, PWDs are provided assistance from job coaches during orientation and safety training.

Central to their commitment to accommodating PWDs is ensuring a good job match between employee knowledge, skills, and abilities, and job interests. Once the match is made, Giant Eagle makes necessary accommodations, which could range from altering tasks or task assignments, to providing equipment, to altering processes. For example, when a deaf employee was hired, he had difficulty using the oven, since a buzzer went off when it was time to remove items. A simple accommodation was implemented by installing a light that flashed when the product was done—inexpensive and effective!

SUMMARY

The development of the rationale for training and hiring people with disabilities came from the emotional intuition that hiring people with disabilities makes sense for the community. While Giovengo identified that some of the tax benefits available to encourage hiring of PWDs were useful, they do not fully offset the additional funds required to adequately train and mentor the employees with disabilities in the jobs that they hold in the company. Many of these costs are also offset by the relatively lower turnover of the employees with disabilities. The supported employment model works for the successful placement and retention of these employees for a long-term employment.[11]

Giant Eagle has won awards for the design of their stores that takes into account accessibility and environmental aspects of the community. The company continues to strive for excellence in the development and execution of the store layout and accessibility for customers as well as employees with disabilities.

By partnering with local nonprofit organizations and schools and providing essential training for persons with disabilities in specific job requirements, Giant Eagle has managed to improve their employee diversity as well as improve their community perception with the hiring of these employees. The requirements of the jobs are matched with the training programs, to ensure success for the hired PWDs.

LESSONS LEARNED

From Giant Eagle's experience in hiring and retaining PWDs, the following lessons may be learned by other companies:

- Partner with local schools to identify and train people with disabilities.
- Develop programs that help PWDs make the transition to employment.
- Use on-the-job training along with job coaches to support PWDs in their employment.
- Obtain union support for flexing rules to accommodate people with disabilities.
- Use nonprofit organizations both for sourcing applicants with disabilities as well as providing quasi-affinity groups for your employees with disabilities.
- Involve nonprofit organizations in the training process. Use their expertise and skills in training your managers and employees.
- Create a people philosophy that supports PWDs.
- Do not compromise hiring standards.
- Do not place arbitrary limits on the jobs that PWDs could do. Focus on their abilities, not their disabilities.

CHAPTER 8

Microsoft

Mark L. Lengnick-Hall

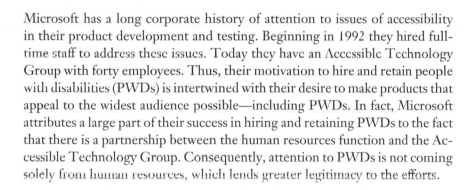

Microsoft has a long corporate history of attention to issues of accessibility in their product development and testing. Beginning in 1992 they hired full-time staff to address these issues. Today they have an Accessible Technology Group with forty employees. Thus, their motivation to hire and retain people with disabilities (PWDs) is intertwined with their desire to make products that appeal to the widest audience possible—including PWDs. In fact, Microsoft attributes a large part of their success in hiring and retaining PWDs to the fact that there is a partnership between the human resources function and the Accessible Technology Group. Consequently, attention to PWDs is not coming solely from human resources, which lends greater legitimacy to the efforts.

TOP MANAGEMENT SUPPORT

Microsoft's efforts to hire and retain PWDs have obtained top management support from Bill Gates. In 1999, Gates along with other business leaders from 21 companies helped to form the Able to Work Consortium (www.nbdc.com), an independent business consortium dedicated to increasing employment opportunities for PWDs. His active and public role in support of hiring PWDs has helped to establish a disability-friendly culture throughout Microsoft. Gates and top management stress that knowledge and skills are most important at Microsoft—having a disability is not an issue if a person has the skills.

Microsoft has found success with five major initiatives directed at hiring and retaining people with disabilities: (1) the establishment of employee/affinity

groups, (2) targeted recruiting, (3) multifaceted training programs and resources, (4) a systematic process for reasonable accommodations, and (5)
creating an early pipeline to identify and attract talented PWDs. Together
these initiatives provide a comprehensive approach to hiring and retaining
PWDs.

MAKING THE BUSINESS CASE FOR HIRING PWDs

Microsoft views people with disabilities as an integral part of the company,
and that people from different disability communities—like people from different ethnic cultures—provide them with valuable perspectives on how they
develop products and services, how they market them, and how they can improve customer satisfaction.[1] At Microsoft, they believe that having employees
with disabilities helps ensure that their products will be useable by the greatest
number of customers. Some examples of how having employees with disabilities contribute to their bottom line follow[2]:

- A blind software test engineer, who holds five patents for accessibility in
  software design, leads Microsoft's assistive device compatibility effort.
- A deaf Encarta Managing Editor realized that adding captions to audio
  files would make it easier for people who are deaf or hard-of-hearing to
  use the product. As a result, Encarta is now close-captioned.
- A Development Lead spends much of his day writing software code using
  voice recognition software and a mouth-stick, because he is a person with
  quadriplegia. As a developer, he is always looking for ways to improve the
  accessibility of Microsoft software.

These examples, and more like them, show that hiring PWDs at Microsoft is
a business decision—and a good one at that!

EMPLOYEE/AFFINITY GROUPS

Employee/affinity groups are self-organized groups that consist of other
employees with similar disabilities. Microsoft has three such employee groups
devoted to PWDs: HUDDLE (deaf and hard-of-hearing), MS ADD (attention deficit disorders), and MS VP (visually impaired persons). These
groups provide support and networking opportunities for PWDs, such as

mentoring, college recruiting, working in the community, career development, and cultural awareness. Each group has an executive sponsor. In addition, each employee group has connections with community groups that are advocates for PWDs. Besides providing social and career support for employees with disabilities, employee groups also help with accessibility and testing of Microsoft products.

TARGETED RECRUITING

Targeted recruiting of people with disabilities involves interactions with advocacy groups such as the Able to Work Consortium, participation in job fairs such as the Hire Disability Job Fair, and college recruiting at traditional colleges for PWDs, such as Galludet University and the National Technical Institute for the Deaf (NTID). Microsoft also places job advertisements in publications targeted to PWDs, such as *Careers and the Disabled*, *Ability Magazine*, and *Diversity Careers in Engineering*. By identifying sources of employees with disabilities, Microsoft is able to identify hidden talent that their competitors may ignore.

MULTIPLE TRAINING PROGRAMS

In addition to targeting their recruiting efforts, Microsoft provides many different training programs that address PWDs. Microsoft trains their recruiting staff to deal with people with disabilities (i.e., disability etiquette training), and additionally provides online resources for recruiters to consult for how to ask specific interview questions. They also interweave issues related to PWDs into their management training programs.

Perhaps their most unique program involves a holistic, process-oriented approach to integrating people with disabilities into their workforce. Prior to the arrival of a new employee with a disability—or shortly after arrival—Microsoft provides opportunities for future coworkers to have their questions about disabilities addressed in an open and safe environment. For those coworkers who have not worked with PWDs, allowing them to satisfy their curiosities goes a long way toward creating a receptive environment. This sensitization process may involve exercises, such as the "silent lunch," in which employees have lunch without talking—forcing them to learn to communicate without speech. This is particularly valuable in sensitizing coworkers to issues regarding working with deaf employees.

New employee orientation provides information to all employees about the valuable contributions that PWDs make in the workplace. During orientation, employees are encouraged to contact the Benefits department if they need job accommodations and they are also provided with ergonomics training.

Besides training to sensitize employees in general to issues of working with PWDs, Microsoft also provides tailored training for dealing with specific disabilities. For example, prior to the arrival of a deaf coworker, one unit was provided training in sign language. This training proved successful not only in preparing employees in the unit for their deaf coworker, but it had other spin-off effects as well. It served as a team-building experience for the group, and those members of the group who had babies at home found that they could communicate through signing with them before they were able to talk.

A SYSTEMATIC APPROACH TO JOB ACCOMMODATIONS

Microsoft takes a systematic approach to providing PWDs with job accommodations. Accommodations are made both for applicants in the hiring process as well as employees at work. Microsoft has found that maintaining a centralized budget for reasonable accommodations allays concerns of hiring managers that are trying to keep their labor costs within limits. Without a centralized budget, there might be a subtle disincentive not to hire a PWD for fear of incurring excessive costs.

In addition to a centralized accommodation budget, Microsoft also has an ADA Accommodations Committee. This committee meets monthly and is given the responsibility of coordinating accommodations throughout the company, discussing the potential impact of new technologies, and evaluating current accommodation programs. Moreover, Microsoft has an Assistive Technologies Team that makes approximately 20 evaluations a month, and an Ergonomics Team that makes approximately 180 one-on-one evaluations a month, spending six to eight hours with each employee evaluated. At their Accessibility Lab, Microsoft employees can try out accommodations before they are implemented.

ATTRACTING YOUNG PWDs

Microsoft believes that identifying and attracting talented PWDs when they are young creates a pipeline of exceptional employees when they are older. To support this objective, Microsoft has numerous programs for young PWDs: job shadowing, career days, internships, scholarships, curriculum development, campus visits, panel discussions with Microsoft employees who have disabilities, and software donations. Microsoft also sponsors a Federal Internship Program in which PWDs receive eleven-week paid internships with federal agencies in Washington, D.C.

SUMMARY

In summary, Microsoft uses a multifaceted approach to hiring and retaining PWDs: top management support, employee/affinity groups, targeted recruiting, multifaceted training, a centralized job accommodation budget and process, and an early pipeline to identify and attract talented PWDs. Their success is symbolized in the story of a deaf college intern from the east coast that chose Microsoft over other companies (and his more familiar geographical environment), because Microsoft offered the most overall support for him to achieve his career goals.

LESSONS LEARNED

From Microsoft's experience in hiring and retaining PWDs, the following lessons may be learned by other companies:

- Top managers must emphasize their support for hiring PWDs in tangible, visible ways.
- Do not make the effort come solely from human resources. Link it to the business case and bottom line. Show why hiring PWDs makes good business sense.
- Focus on accessibility of products for both customers with disabilities as well as employees with disabilities.
- Make it possible for PWDs to connect with each other throughout the organization for social and emotional support.
- Provide recruiters training on recruiting and interviewing for people with specific types of disabilities.
- Provide coworkers both general sensitivity training and specific training for particular disabilities.

- Eliminate disincentives for making reasonable accommodations by having a centralized accommodation budget.
- Coordinate reasonable accommodations throughout the company.
- Develop an early pipeline to locate and attract PWD talent.
- Use a multifaceted approach to hiring and retaining PWDs.

CHAPTER 9

Marriott International

Robert R. Hull

Marriott is somewhat unique in that it is a very large, international corporation that is so proactive it has created its own operating foundation. In 2004, the Marriott Foundation for People with Disabilities and its programs, *Bridges from School to Work* and *Bridges Plus*, won the New Freedom Initiative Award presented by the U.S. Department of Labor. The Marriott Foundation was formed in 1989, four years after the death of the corporation's founder, J. Willard Marriott. The Foundation's website credits "the Marriott family" with the motivation for its work with people with disabilities, and indeed, Alice Sheets Marriott, wife of the founder, served many years on national boards of the Arthritis Foundation and Goodwill Industries International, while the founder's son, J.W. Marriott, Jr., serves as Chairman of both Marriott International and the Marriott Foundation.[1]

Marriott Corporation has been a leader in providing disability access in its hotels long before the advent of the Americans with Disabilities Act. According to Chairman Richard Marriott, their involvement is motivated by a broader interest in making their company, their communities, and their country stronger and more productive.[2] While the company does enjoy the benefits of tax incentives for hiring people with disabilities (PWDs), this has not been their primary motivation for their efforts. In fact, during the company's growth period in the 1980s and 1990s, PWDs were considered a valuable source of labor in tight markets.

Marriott has been involved in many partnerships with organizations that assist people with disabilities to enter the workforce. Most of their operations have local connections with community-based organizations working with people with disabilities. For example, 20 years ago, the New York Marriott Marquis in Manhattan hired a large number of hearing-impaired associates. This was accomplished through a partnership with local community-based disability organizations.

BRIDGES FROM SCHOOL TO WORK *AND* BRIDGES PLUS

The Marriott Corporation established a separate nonprofit organization to assist youth with disabilities in entering the workplace. The Marriott Foundation for People with Disabilities has a renowned program called "Bridges" which links young people leaving high school special education programs with local businesses through competitive job placements.[3]

Executives of the Marriott Corporation often serve on the boards of the *Bridges* projects; associates (employees) frequently offer volunteer time and skills; and key Foundation events such as employer luncheons and project graduations are held at the hotels. The Foundation creates *Bridges* projects in cities where the corporation has multiple hotels; currently *Bridges* projects operate in Atlanta; Chicago; Dallas; Fairfax County, Virginia; Los Angeles; Montgomery County, Maryland; San Francisco; and Washington, D.C. Since their inception in 1990, the *Bridges* projects have placed more than 8,500 youth with disabilities aged 17–22 with more than 1,500 employers. Somewhat surprisingly, the *Bridges* projects are not significant feeders of employees to the corporation's hotels, as Marriott International prefers to hire employees aged 21 and older.

THE BRIDGES PROGRAM

The Bridges program was founded in 1989 and its initial design was guided by employer focus groups. Marriott wanted to share with the broader business community the lessons learned relative to the employment of PWDs. And, most important, this program was developed of, by, and for business. There was intent to make a partnership with business at the core of all activities.

The Bridges program has three main objectives: (1) to prepare youth with disabilities for the workplace and provide ongoing assistance with job search, attainment, and retention; (2) to promote to employers the benefits of hiring from this pool of potential employees; and (3) to provide support to employers in the recruitment, hiring, and retention of youth with disabilities.

The Bridges program is based on fundamental guiding principles. First, while striving to enhance the employment prospects of youth with disabilities, Bridges is focused on meeting the workforce needs of employers. Second, Bridges employs an efficient and effective strategy in which one capable professional, rather than a cadre of specialists, delivers services that are individualized, flexible, and competency-based. Third, each research-based program component is guided by the premise that employment success will occur when three conditions are met: (1) the job is well matched to the applicant's skills, experience, and interests; (2) both employee and employer are committed and prepared to work effectively with each other; and (3) appropriate supports are provided to all parties, especially early in the employment experience.

THE BRIDGES PLUS PROGRAM

The Bridges Plus program focuses more specifically on career development. For each youth enrolled, they create a Career Development Plan that guides all activities for two years and employ 90-day reviews and action planning to ensure progress toward vocational goals. Another component of the Bridges Plus program is the Career Preparation Curriculum. This curriculum contains essential competencies for career development, self-advocacy, and successful employment. Learning is tailored to the individual youth's needs and capabilities. The final component of the Bridges Plus program is the employer representative. Employer representatives provide mentoring, supportive services, and family training. This is designed to provide the participants with a competitive work experience leading to vocational growth and advancement as well as economic self-sufficiency.

BENEFITS OF THE BRIDGES AND BRIDGES PLUS PROGRAMS

The Bridges program and the Bridges Plus program provide benefits to both employers and PWDs. Employers benefit from the program by obtaining (a) a rich new pool of applicants who have been pre-screened to meet their critical, core job needs, (b) applicants who have received job readiness training prior to placement, and (c) applicants who are being supported to approach the placement as a long-term commitment to vocational success and growth—not a short-term source of income. PWDs benefit from the program by receiving (a) entry to work opportunities, with the potential for long-term success, and

(b) ongoing interventions by project staff to assure that services and supports necessary for that success are available to them, and (c) guidance in developing a career plan specific to their skills and objectives with intermediate action steps to assure success.

PRACTICING WHAT THEY PREACH

Marriott International is a management and franchising corporation. The hotel properties are owned by private investors who are franchisees of the Marriott operations, including all human resource management. Marriott International has had a large training program for decades. When the Americans with Disabilities Act (ADA) became law in 1990, the training department incorporated the new expectations into their ongoing management training.[4] This included "hiring expectations, reasonable accommodations, modifications in the buildings, and other changes."[5] Over the 15 years since the enactment of the ADA, Marriott's policy of internal advancement has meant these expectations have permeated the organizational culture.

In 1999, Marriott established another program—Pathways to Independence—to teach PWDs with visual impairments and veterans the needed skills to obtain and retain jobs.[6] This innovative program focuses on communication skills, appropriate workplace behavior, strong work ethic, dependability, accountability, and addressing personal challenges. Participants must receive 60 hours of classroom instruction and 120 hours of occupational training. Both classroom and occupational training are conducted at a Marriott business by Marriott managers and supervisors. Participants are not considered employees of Marriott, and they do not receive wages or benefits while in the program. Furthermore, trainees do not displace any current Marriott employees, or cause a reduction in employee work hours—thus not creating any perceived inequities among current employees. Once the participants successfully complete the program, they are placed in full-time positions, with benefits, at a Marriott business. Thus, this program provides training and a job tryout before hiring PWDs.

As new dimensions of the ADA have come to the forefront, Marriott takes a proactive, leadership stance in engaging with them. Currently, training is focusing on accessibility issues for customers with disabilities who use service animals; indeed, Marriott's training division has published a training guide for a video on the issue produced by the California Hotel Association Educational Foundation.[7] Marriott works on such issues nationally as an active member of the National Business and Disability Council.

As with any large employer, there is some unevenness in the employment record. While there are only a scattering of executive managers with disabilities, the company points to two instances of "natural clustering": the opening of the Marriott Marquis in New York City in 1986 had an unusually large number of new employees with hearing impairments, while in Santa Ana, California, a reservation call center employs more than 25 individuals with visual impairments, including the general manager.[8] Local managers' hiring initiatives thus seem to be well received within the company.

CHANGING PERCEPTUAL FRAMES

In addition to the Bridges and Bridges Plus programs, changing perceptual frames has been a consistent theme in Marriott's approach to hiring and retaining PWDs. This occurs in several ways. One, managers are encouraged to set aside their preconceptions of PWDs and think creatively about reasonable accommodations. Often this simply involves allowing PWDs to explain how they believe they can perform the job. As chairman Marriott points out, most accommodations are simple and inexpensive, such as the use of wooden blocks to raise a work station. Second, working with community organizations can also overcome mistaken preconceptions about necessary accommodations and their expense. For example, one hotel manager wanted to find a way to communicate with a hearing impaired employee. Rather than implementing an expensive paging system, working with the community-based organization they were able to identify a cheaper, but equally effective, solution—use a cell phone with text messaging and a vibrator function. Three, managers are trained to explain accommodations to coworkers of PWDs by emphasizing that anyone—including them—may someday need an accommodation at work.

Marriott also makes efforts to match PWDs with jobs that they are able to perform. For example, at their reservation center in California, the manager of the unit is visually impaired, as are the employees. Accommodations are easily fitted to these employees to overcome the constraints of their disabilities. On the other hand, visually impaired employees would not be as good a fit in server jobs at Marriott's restaurants.

One issue that emerged with the ADA was managers' perceptions of lesser productivity from job candidates with disabilities. "What we try to train is that, rather than overlaying your assumptions about their abilities or lack of abilities, just try to let them explain how they will do that job. You may not have ever thought about how to do it in another manner ... [you should] work at the dialogue to see if that is a possibility."[9]

Just as hiring managers needed to be trained in the company's expectations of their openness to new possibilities for accomplishing the job, so other coworkers have at times needed additional training. The potential problems of coworkers' judgments of fairness are present in such a large employee workforce. When a manager makes what he or she determines to be a reasonable accommodation, the ADA proscribes discussing the decision with anyone but the individual employee affected, for reasons of confidentiality. This accommodation decision may or may not appear to other coworkers as fair to them, resulting in questioning or resentment. Marriott indicates that "our response is to teach our managers to say, 'Look, you know I need to work with this individual according to the law and you just need to trust that I am making a well-founded decision. If you needed something, we would work through what your needs were as well."[10]

Thus the issue of perceived fairness of various accommodations seems to be lessened when managers are trained to be accommodating across the board—no employee can predict when a temporary illness or a need to care for a family member will arise and mean they need flexibility or accommodation from their employer as well.

There was also some indication of the "radiation" of various accommodations to other employees; for example, senior executives who are older often use larger fonts on their computers, a disability accessibility feature developed by Microsoft and other software providers to accommodate visual impairment.[11]

Marriott International is quite evidently proud of their relationships with the business and human services organizations in the communities where they locate their hotels, as well as their national and international reputation. Local community relations include, for example, "CEOs of disability organizations," who are invited along with other business leaders to meetings in the hotels. From these relationships has come the knowledge of other business leaders about both Marriott International's proactive hiring practices and the Foundation's *Bridges* program's success with its graduates. Current Marriott International/Foundation chairperson Richard E. Marriott often is the keynote speaker at these events. From the community disability organizations, the Marriott hotels often obtain help with accommodation issues, and in turn host job coaches who assist employees with disabilities.[12]

SUMMARY

In summary, Marriott Corporation has experienced success in hiring and retaining PWDs through efforts by local units that establish relationships with community-based disability organizations and match people to jobs that can be performed with accommodation. In conjunction with their overall diversity efforts, managers are trained to overcome their preconceptions and to think creatively about accommodations. This simple strategy with top management support has proven effective. Moreover, Marriott has taken a leadership role in encouraging other businesses to hire and retain PWDs through its Bridges program.

LESSONS LEARNED

From Marriott's experience in hiring and retaining PWDs, the following lessons may be learned by other companies:

- Take a socially responsible perspective on hiring PWDs.
- Share what you have learned about hiring PWDs with other employers.
- Change the perceptual frames toward PWDs.
- Encourage managers to think creatively about reasonable accommodations.
- Work with community-based organizations to find less costly but effective accommodations.
- Have managers explain accommodations to coworkers of the PWDs.
- Match PWDs to jobs they can perform.

SECTION THREE

Lessons Learne
Retaining Peopl

CHAPTER 10

The Business Case for Hiring People with Disabilities

Mark L. Lengnick-Hall

Many employers and managers are reluctant to hire people with disabilities (PWDs) because they fear that the costs of these employees will outweigh the benefits. On the cost side, employers may believe that employees with disabilities will incur greater expenses than nondisabled employees, such as the cost of job accommodations and greater health care costs. On the benefits side, employers may believe that employees with disabilities will not be as productive as their nondisabled counterparts. When they put the two parts of the equation together—increased costs and decreased benefits—employers may believe that hiring PWDs simply is not a sound business decision.

In fact, a good business case can be made for hiring PWDs. There are many sound business reasons for hiring and retaining PWDs and they will be discussed next.

ADAPT TO DEMOGRAPHIC INEVITABILITY

Two parallel workforce trends will make hiring and retaining PWDs an effective strategy. There will be a larger number of older people in the workforce and a smaller number of young new entrants to replace them. Here are some projections from the Bureau of Labor Statistics[1]:

- The projected labor force growth will be affected by the aging of the baby boom generation—persons born between 1946 and 1964.

- In 2014, baby boomers will be ages 50 to 68 years, and this age group will grow significantly over the 2004–2014 period.

- The labor force will continue to age, with the number of workers in the 55-and-older group projected to grow by 49.1%, nearly 5 times the 10% growth projected for the overall labor force.

- Youths—those between the ages of 16 and 24—will decline in numbers and lose share of the labor force, from 15.1% in 2004 to 13.7% in 2014.

- Prime-age workers—those between the ages of 25 and 54—also will lose share of the labor force, from 69.3% in 2004 to 65.2% in 2014.

- The 55-and-older age group, on the other hand, is projected to gain share of the labor force, from 15.6% to 21.2%.

The aging of the workforce means there will be more employees with disabilities in the future. As baby boomers age, growing numbers of them will experience physical impairments, creating accessibility challenges and the need for employers to find ways to provide accommodations. Consequently, providing technology and other accommodations that help valued employees remain productive for a longer period of time makes good business sense. By prolonging the period that employees can be productive—even with disabilities—employers will be able to obtain a greater rate of return on their employees. Both hiring PWDs and retaining employees who become disabled is one way that organizations can meet their workforce needs both now and in the future.

In addition to aging baby boomers that will experience disabilities, large numbers of people will experience temporary impairments caused by illness and accident that affect their ability to do their jobs. Organizations that have the capacity to return these employees to work faster and accommodate them so they can be productive will have an advantage over competitors who do not have that capacity.

Becoming disabled (either temporarily or permanently) can happen to anyone at any time. By taking a more proactive stance toward hiring and retaining PWDs, employers will be able both to take advantage of this valuable talent pool today and be prepared to retain and reap the benefits of productive employees who become disabled in the future.

INCREASE RETENTION AND REDUCE TURNOVER

Turnover is expensive for organizations. It can cost upwards to 150% or more of annual salary to replace an employee, so there is a large out of pocket expense.[2] However, more costly may be the loss of organizational knowledge when even a single employee leaves. Since employees are embedded in social systems within their organizations, there are negative ripple effects when someone leaves the organization, disrupting organizational functioning. Therefore, retaining valued employees negates the high cost of hiring and training replacements, and in addition improves organizational functioning by maintaining productive social systems.

There is much anecdotal evidence and some research support that indicates PWDs are loyal, committed workers, and less likely to turnover than their nondisabled counterparts.[3] For example, Hire Potential discovered that employees with disabilities were more committed and retained on average 50% longer than traditional workers. Marriott found that employees with disabilities hired through their Pathways to Independence program had a 6% turnover rate in comparison to a 52% turnover rate for their overall workforce. Pizza Hut has experienced retention rates four to five times higher for their employees with disabilities in comparison to their nondisabled employees. Consequently, by hiring PWDs, organizations may lower turnover, reduce costs (for hiring and training replacements), and increase organizational effectiveness (through maintaining stable subunits where organizational knowledge is retained and enhanced).

ENHANCE PRODUCTIVITY

By creating an environment that helps integrate PWDs, organizations also enhance the productivity of all employees. Solving accessibility problems for PWDs has the spin-off benefit of enhancing productivity for nondisabled employees, too. This is due to the fact that many jobs and workplaces are designed to take into account technical and operational considerations more so than human considerations. Nondisabled employees may be able to more easily perform jobs that are not optimally designed in work environments that also are not optimally designed. However, by making something (tasks, processes, etc.) easier for PWDs to do, organizations often make doing something easier for all employees; thus PWDs bring new knowledge to a business. By creating accessibility in jobs and workplaces, employers can make it possible for PWDs as well as nondisabled employees achieve their maximum productivity.

For example, by providing accessible technology (e.g., computers), collaboration and communication among all employees—whether they have a disability or not—can be facilitated, resulting in greater organizational productivity. Accessible technology makes it possible for all employees to share documents, collaborate on projects, and communicate among team members. Providing employees the opportunity to customize their computers (e.g., modify the way information is presented to them—visually, aurally, and tactilely), makes it possible for them to more easily communicate with their colleagues. Furthermore, with productivity software widely available, these employees can also more easily collaborate on projects.

Having PWDs in the workforce can enhance productivity in other ways, too. For example, the experience of working with PWDs can raise the morale of other employees. PWDs overcome challenges and obstacles on a daily basis and provide inspiration and motivation to their nondisabled coworkers. Thus, having PWDs in the work group may raise everyone's expectations for performance.

REDUCE COSTS

By providing an environment that helps integrate PWDs, organizations can reduce costs in four ways: (1) by returning employees with temporary disabilities to work more quickly and efficiently, (2) by reducing turnover costs, (3) by reducing costs of litigation, and (4) by obtaining tax breaks.

First, accessible technology can help reduce costs of time lost and costs incurred when an employee develops a temporary disability by allowing an employee to remain productive and up to date, and it may even prevent an organization from needing to hire a temporary replacement. Accessible technology may allow a worker to, for example, work from home during the recovery period, and thus prevent work from piling up during the absence.

Second, as described earlier, PWDs may have lower turnover rates than their nondisabled counterparts, eliminating the cost of hiring replacements. This both saves the time involved in hiring replacements and getting them up to speed in the job as well as the direct costs associated with finding new employees. Therefore, by hiring PWDs an important source of labor costs can be lowered.

Third, by having a more proactive stance on hiring and retaining PWDs, organizations may be able to avoid costly disability discrimination lawsuits. Even a single case of disability discrimination can be costly to an organization, taking up time of staff in preparing a defense, direct costs for legal representation, court costs, and potential costs associated with losing. In addition, it is difficult to quantify the loss of reputation incurred as a result of a drawn-out legal proceeding that receives media attention. However, one research study found that the announcements of discrimination settlements were associated with significant and negative stock price changes.[4] That is, the stock prices of companies went down as a result of publicly announced discrimination settlements. So, not only is it costly to defend against such discrimination suits, it also is costly to a company's valuation in the stock market. Avoiding such costs through positive organizational practices clearly is a preferred strategy.

Fourth, businesses can take advantage of tax breaks ranging from $2,400 to $15,000 when they hire, retain, or accommodate a PWD (see Appendix 1 for more details of these tax incentives). For example, the Work Opportunity Tax Credit allows employers tax credits of up to $2,400 for hiring people with disabilities; the Small Business Tax Credit helps owners cover the cost of making their small business accessible up to a maximum benefit of $5,000; and businesses can take an annual deduction of up to $15,000 for expenses incurred to remove physical, structural, and transportation barriers for persons with disabilities in the workplace. As a result of these tax incentives, businesses can lower their labor costs by hiring PWDs. In a world of ever-increasing cost competition, tax incentives for productive employees makes hiring PWDs that much more attractive. In addition, by hiring PWDs, fewer people will need SSI (Supplemental Security Income) and SSDI (Supplemental Security Disability Income). This benefits everyone who pays taxes, and since companies bear the greatest tax burden, this lowers their costs.

The economic effect of unemployment of Americans with disabilities in our society is substantial.[5] Direct government and private payments to support people with disabilities of employable age who do not have jobs is estimated to be $232 billion annually and another $195 billion in earnings and taxes are lost each year because Americans with disabilities are unemployed. By comparison, the annual budget deficit of the United States is approximately $200 billion. The more PWDs who can be employed, the lower the costs to society.

ENHANCE RECRUITMENT

Organizations that take active steps to integrate PWDs—both through hiring and retention strategies—create opportunities for themselves to hire the best talent available. On the other hand those organizations that do not actively hire and retain PWDs run the risk of losing talented employees to their competitors. Consequently, hiring and retaining PWDs can be a source of competitive advantage if companies are able to hire better employees (i.e., talented PWDs) who are ignored by their competitors.

Both the image organizations present as well as the employee value proposition they offer largely determine the desire of applicants—both PWDs and the nondisabled—to work for them. An organizational image that emphasizes inclusiveness—and specifically identifies PWDs—certainly will be positively received by applicants with disabilities. PWDs will likely believe that such organizations are both more receptive to them and are places where they will be most likely to make contributions and be rewarded for them. On the other hand, organizations that do not emphasize inclusiveness, and do not have any indicators of receptivity to PWDs, are less likely to be as attractive to applicants with disabilities.

Furthermore, many new entrants into the workforce today (both with and without disabilities) are looking for organizations that have a social conscience and act responsibly.[6] By demonstrating an outreach to all groups—including PWDs—organizations may be better able to show that they are committed to equality and social responsibility. By providing an environment that helps integrate PWDs, organizations may be able to hire the best of applicants— both the best PWDs and the best nondisabled, too.

INCREASE MARKET OPPORTUNITIES

By providing an environment that helps integrate PWDs, organizations can reach a broader customer base and increase their market opportunities. PWDs are an often ignored or underestimated market segment.[7]

- PWDs are a market that consists of approximately 54 million people who have an aggregate income of $1 trillion, of which $220 billion represents discretionary spending power.
- Of the nearly 70 million American families, 20 million have at least one PWD.
- PWDs spent more than $81 billion on travel in 1995.
- It has also been estimated that a 12% increase in revenues in the hotel and hospitality industry is due to PWDs who have better access to these businesses as a result of the Americans with Disabilities Act.

In addition, the World Health Organization estimates that there are 600 million PWDs worldwide, meaning the global market for PWDs is substantial.[8]

With this much buying power and the need for products and services that are accessible, it is no wonder that more and more organizations are hiring PWDs, both to obtain their expertise and knowledge and obtain insights they might not otherwise gain as well as to better relate to their customers with disabilities. Employees with disabilities can also provide insights into the growing market of older customers, since many of them experience impairments that require accessibility and accommodations.

OBTAIN CREATIVE PROBLEM-SOLVING SKILLS

PWDs bring unique perspectives, experiences, and problem-solving skills to the workplace. After all, what it takes to manage a disability—problem-solving, perseverance, planning, and people skills—are all aspects of the human capital an organization needs in order to adapt to changing business environments. Having diversity, such as PWDs, represented in organizational teams and groups can improve decision-making outcomes. For example, heterogeneous groups outperform homogeneous groups in identifying problem perspectives and generating alternative solutions.[9]

Cisco Systems CEO John Chambers is one executive who has realized the value of PWDs for improving creativity.[10] Since some of the company's customers have employees with disabilities, acclimating Cisco's workers to professional contact with employees with disabilities inside the company has the added benefit of enabling them to work productively with the company's clients.

GENERATE GOODWILL

Hiring and retaining PWDs is viewed by both customers and employees as an important way a company can give something back to the community. This goodwill that is fostered by the company enhances its reputation and is a positive influence in attracting new employees and new customers. People want to work for companies that have good reputations in the community; they also want to buy products and services from these companies.

Researchers at the Center for Social Development and Education at the University of Massachusetts Boston found an overwhelmingly positive attitude among consumers toward socially responsible companies, and in particular toward those that hire individuals with disabilities.[11] Ninety-two percent of consumers surveyed felt more favorable toward companies that hire individuals with disabilities, and 87% said they would prefer to give their business to such companies. Furthermore, among those surveyed, hiring people with disabilities ranked third behind offering health insurance to all employees and protecting the environment as an indicator of a company's commitment to social justice.

Having effective diversity programs, such as those for PWDs, may also positively affect a company's stock price. In examining the stock price changes before and after the announcement of the U.S. Department of Labor's Exemplary Voluntary Efforts Award (recognizing firms with high quality diversity programs), researchers found significant and positive excess returns.[12] The message is clear—doing the right thing is good business.

SUMMARY

A compelling business case for hiring and retaining PWDs can indeed be made and it is necessary to do so to persuade some skeptics. Stereotypes, prejudices, and preconceptions often get in the way of clear-headed decision making about human resources. This seems to be even truer for PWDs. Without factual information about PWDs and how they can be integrated into the workplace, many PWDs will be routinely screened out from jobs they not only could do, but could do so exceedingly well. This is a loss for the PWD who doesn't obtain employment, a loss for the organization that doesn't obtain a talented employee, and the loss for society that bears the costs for unemployment.

CHAPTER 11

Creating a Disability-Friendly Organizational Culture and Climate

Mark L. Lengnick-Hall

What can be learned from these seven leading companies about how to attract, retain, and benefit from people with disabilities (PWDs)? There are some commonalities and some differences in how they approach this issue. These organizations have in common the need to create organizational change—getting managers and employees to overcome prejudices and stereotypes about PWDs and move toward viewing them as valuable organizational resources. Furthermore, changing how employees and managers think about PWDs is only part of the solution; they also have to change their behaviors. However, the particular ingredients of that organizational change depend upon particular organizational characteristics. For example, the larger companies like Microsoft and SunTrust Banks have more resources and formalized structures, while the small manufacturing company A&F Wood Products has fewer resources and uses a more informal approach that relies heavily upon community-based disability organizations. That is, while there is no one best way to hire, retain, and benefit from PWDs, there appears to be some effective approaches that could—and should—be tailored to fit particular organizational circumstances. This chapter will present a model of organizational change and show how the programs, practices, and policies of the organizations profiled in this book have been used to improve the employment and utilization of PWDs.

WHAT IS A DISABILITY-FRIENDLY CULTURE AND CLIMATE?

Culture refers to an organization's broad pattern of mores, values, and beliefs.[1] For many companies, culture reflects the mores, values, and beliefs of their founders. Over time, organizational culture may evolve or change (e.g., after the founder dies), but if companies are successful, these mores, values, and beliefs may continue to provide direction and guidance. Jim Collins describes in his book *Built to Last*[2] companies with strong cultures derived from their founders that have endured over decades. Thus, culture involves firmly implanted beliefs and values of organizational members that reside at a deeper level of people's psychology. It is a more subtle psychology of the workplace—not tangible, but below the surface.[3] For example, Hewlett-Packard (one of the companies profiled in this book) on their website identify the following written by cofounders Bill Hewlett and Dave Packard as their corporate objectives that have guided the company in the conduct of its business since 1957: "It is necessary that people work together in unison toward common objectives and avoid working at cross purposes at all levels if the ultimate in efficiency and achievement is to be obtained." This simple, but elegant, expression of the mores, values, and beliefs (i.e., the culture) has made Hewlett-Packard a world leader in the computer industry.

Climate, on the other hand, is more tangible and more visible. It is the manifestation of an organization's culture. Climate is the atmosphere that employees perceive. It is how an organization feels. It is created by practices, procedures, and rewards.[4] Climate is created more by what management does as opposed to what it says. For example, management may say that it rewards performance but actually practices favoritism to particular individuals or groups. The climate experienced by employees—that atmosphere they perceive in the example—is one that cronyism is more important than job performance. Thus, it is important that management take great care in ensuring that the climate it espouses is that which it actually implements.

Many organizations have cultures that ostensibly are inclusive and proclaim such worthy values as "our people are our most important asset," "we hire the best people," "hard work and effort are what counts," and "everyone has an equal opportunity to get a job and move up in our organization if they are qualified and perform their jobs well." For many people who apply for and get jobs at these companies, the values indeed reflect the culture they encounter. This is true for a larger number of people today who historically have been excluded from employment, such as minorities and women. However, despite the inclusive tone of values adopted by many corporations, many continue to provide obstacles and barriers to PWDs. Subtle and unintentional practices, procedures, and reward systems (i.e., aspects of climate) create unnecessary roadblocks that many PWDs cannot overcome. For example, job descriptions may be written that imply there is only one way of accomplishing tasks (and that way assumes no disability) and may inadvertently deter a PWD from applying for a job or deter a hiring supervisor from considering a PWD for employment. Coworker fears that PWDs may mean extra work or loss of productivity rewards may make them reluctant to welcome a PWD as a colleague. These fears may be justified if the climate produced by management's practices and procedures make their fears a reality.

A disability-friendly culture may best be described as one that has a value of focusing on ability and not disability, equal opportunity, and treating all employees fairly. That is, the organization focuses on valuing what an individual can do, not what she cannot do. Equal opportunity implies that PWDs have a chance to perform any job that they are capable of performing; it doesn't imply that they can perform any job, just that they have the opportunity. Fair treatment implies that PWDs are not arbitrarily discriminated against based upon negative (e.g., he can't possibly do that job) or positive (e.g., she shouldn't do that job because it might be dangerous for her) biases. These characteristics of a disability-friendly culture would likely be embraced by anyone—with or without a disability.

In creating a disability-friendly climate, organizations are most likely to encounter a host of problems and potential points of resistance. These problems likely derive from the way organizations historically have obtained and used their human resources. Going back to the earliest days of the industrial era, employees were selected based on their physical health and abilities, and jobs were designed around people who had no disabilities.[5] For example, in a manufacturing setting, if an employee experienced an industrial accident resulting in a physical disability, he could no longer perform the job and would be terminated. Because of this historical precedence, many managers and employees have come to think of the workplace as one in which you must be healthy and have few, if any, disabilities. The emergence and evolution of government supports for PWDs, through programs such as Social Security, have further reinforced stereotypes that PWDs cannot work, and should just be supported by other means. For many employees and managers, these perceptions are not destructive in their motivation, but they are in their behaviors—inadvertently leading, in many cases, to unfair discrimination.

A disability-friendly climate is one that uses practices, procedures, and rewards to create an atmosphere such that employees and managers perceive the following:

• It is important to provide everyone—including PWDs—opportunities for employment and career development.

- It is important to hold everyone—including PWDs—accountable for making substantial contributions to organizational performance.

- Anyone can acquire a disability at any time—so how we treat PWDs reflects how we would like to be treated ourselves if we become temporarily or permanently disabled.

As described in more detail below, the leading companies profiled in this book have developed and used practices and procedures that can facilitate progress toward a disability-friendly climate.

A MODEL OF ORGANIZATIONAL CHANGE

Kurt Lewin first proposed a model of planned organizational change in the 1950s.[6] Since then, his model has been expanded upon (e.g., Schein[7]), but remained very robust for both explaining organizational change and providing a roadmap of how to do it. Lewin's model of planned organizational change proposes that there are three stages: unfreezing, moving, and refreezing.

In the first stage—*unfreezing*—organizations must create a felt need for change. That is, there must be a reason(s) for doing it and it must be such that it is convincing to the majority of organizational members. The reason could be an external pressure, such as a change in consumer demand that forces an organization to reexamine its business model. Alternatively, the reasons could come from within the organization, such as a change in strategy. To unfreeze the organization, it is necessary to challenge beliefs, values, attitudes, and behaviors that employees and managers currently hold. Resistance to change is most likely to occur at this stage.

In the second stage—*moving*—the change itself is implemented. Depending upon the type of change that is implemented, this usually involves top management directives and various programs to move the organization to its desired new state. Employees and managers need guidance in what they are supposed to do and how they are supposed to behave. This stage can take some time depending upon the size of the organization and the amount and type of change.

And finally, in the third stage—*refreezing*—after the change has been implemented, it must become institutionalized as a new way of doing things. Practices, procedures, and policies are put in place to lock in the new desired organizational state. At this stage, employees and managers have embraced the change (or become resigned to it), and conduct their daily affairs in the new and desired ways.

The eight companies profiled in this book either explicitly or implicitly used the model of planned organizational change in their efforts to hire, retain, and benefit from PWDs. Next, each stage of the model of planned organizational change will be examined in more detail and examples from the companies profiled in this book will be used to illustrate how it can be applied to employing PWDs.

UNFREEZING

Getting employees and managers to embrace a change to hiring, retaining, and utilizing PWDs is different from triggers that typically are cited as examples of unfreezing organizations. Typical examples involve declining sales, threatened bankruptcies, customer dissatisfaction, and the like. Expanding recruitment and hiring to include more PWDs rarely has the same aura of crisis, prompting organizational members to give their collective nod of acceptance. One exception described in this book is A&F Wood Products, a company that was desperate for employees as it sought expanded distribution for its products. Because of its rural location, and local labor market conditions, a labor shortage crisis of sorts made unfreezing from current hiring practices easy to sell. On the other hand, larger organizations, like Microsoft and Hewlett-Packard, had to use different means for unfreezing their organizations. By focusing on the large potential market for their products among customers with disabilities, they were able to sell the need to hire PWDs in order to better take advantage of that opportunity.

There are four steps that organizations can take to ensure that the unfreezing stage goes smoothly[8]: (1) determine what needs to change, (2) ensure that there is strong support from upper management, (3) create the need for change, and (4) understand and address the doubts and concerns of managers and employees.

DETERMINE WHAT NEEDS TO CHANGE

In the case of hiring PWDs, several factors likely need to change in most organizations. For one, employees and managers need to change their attitudes. Many people who do not have disabilities hold incorrect assumptions about what PWDs can do in the workplace. Furthermore, they do not value the potential contributions that PWDs could make in the workplace. While this is largely an issue of educating employees and managers about facts versus stereotypes, it is nonetheless a critical hurdle that must be overcome. Similarly, behaviors need to change. Oftentimes, employees and managers simply don't know how to behave around people with disabilities. Awkward and unfortunate behaviors may lead to misunderstandings. Again, educating employees and managers can go a long way toward solving this problem.

ENSURE THERE IS STRONG SUPPORT FROM TOP MANAGEMENT

Research has shown that top management support can make the difference between success and failure of many types of programs.[9] It seems that top management support is especially critical in encouraging change to embrace hiring and retaining PWDs. Since many employees may not see how hiring and working with PWDs will benefit them or the company per se, a directive from top management perhaps can change behaviors before attitudes come around. Top management support is evident in all of the companies profiled in this book. Their support for hiring and retaining PWDs is both tangible and visible. Some companies, for example SunTrust Bank, assign top managers to lead the hiring efforts and report their progress and accomplishments in their annual reports. One characteristic of top management support is the necessity for emphasizing a business case for hiring PWDs and framing it as warranting organization-wide importance, and not simply espousing a socially desirable corporate behavior.

CREATE THE NEED FOR CHANGE

Hiring PWDs is part of an organization's larger diversity efforts. The companies in this book emphasize PWDs as one of the groups of people that their diversity efforts target. This is made clear in numerous corporate communications and on their websites. The need for change is made most clear when companies argue that diversity in general—and hiring PWDs in particular—opens up new markets and has the potential to positively influence the bottom line. For example, the former Chairman and CEO of Hewlett-Packard said the following: "From the beginning of our reinvention, we said that all our actions would be aimed at connecting people to the power of technology, harnessing it to lift human potential. In keeping that promise, HP made a commitment to provide leadership in designing accessible products and services for people with disabilities." The simple logic is that by making products and services more accessible, a company can reach a broader market and become more profitable and competitive. By hiring PWDs, companies gain expert knowledge on how to market their products and services to customers with disabilities. In addition, by having PWDs in prominent positions, companies are more attractive to customers with disabilities. By aligning diversity initiatives in general, and PWD initiatives in particular, with business strategy, the companies in this book demonstrate how to effectively create the need for change.

UNDERSTAND AND ADDRESS THE DOUBTS AND CONCERNS OF MANAGERS AND EMPLOYEES

Managers and coworkers likely have doubts about whether PWDs can do the job and concerns about how having PWDs in their units will affect productivity, pay, and other important personal and group outcomes. Perhaps the best way to attack this issue is directly. For example, Giant Eagle makes it clear that they will not lower hiring standards or job performance expectations for PWDs. They make it clear to managers and coworkers that PWDs who are hired by the company are carefully screened for qualifications, provided pre-entry training, carefully matched to jobs they can perform, and provided necessary accommodations to do their jobs. At A&F Wood Products, top management addresses doubts and concerns in a unique way. They remind coworkers and supervisors that anyone could become disabled—including them. By personalizing the concerns, A&F Wood Products helps reduce resistance to the change.

MOVING

Once unfrozen, organizations can begin taking steps to implement the desired change. The first step involves choosing where to start. Efforts to improve the employment of PWDs can begin either at the top, at the bottom, or even from both directions. It helps when an organization has a disability philosophy to guide and direct efforts in the way a mission or vision statement provides direction for an organization's overall strategy. Larger organizations can set up temporary organizational structures to get the change effort off the ground and more permanent structures to sustain their efforts over time.

USE TOP-DOWN AND BOTTOM-UP CHANGE INITIATIVES

These change efforts may begin at the top and filter down the organization. Microsoft is a good example of top management (specifically Bill Gates) deciding to increase the employment of PWDs and communicating that directive to all units within the organization. The top-down approach clearly has the advantage of authority and may cause behavioral change before attitudes change—after all, managers and employees must comply with directives from the top.

On the other hand, change efforts may begin at the bottom and filter upward in the organization. SunTrust Bank is a good example of this approach. An employee at one of their field offices had the knowledge and skill to use sign language, identified an opportunity for expanding services to deaf customers (and later customers with other disabilities), and as word spread throughout the company of that office's success in generating new business, other field offices began providing similar services. The bottom-up approach has the advantage of providing proof that those efforts to hire and retain PWDs pay off, and thus changes attitudes before behaviors change.

DEVELOP A DISABILITY PHILOSOPHY

A simple, but powerful, disability philosophy can provide focus and direction for an organization's efforts. Two companies in this book exemplify how this can be enacted. Both A&F Wood Products and Giant Eagle Supermarkets espouse a philosophy of "ability, not disability." At A&F Wood Products, a blind employee was not prevented from operating dangerous manufacturing machinery; instead her supervisor used his creativity to develop job accommodations to make it possible. Similarly, at Giant Eagle Supermarkets, employees with a range of disabilities (deafness, hearing impairment, blindness, vision impairment, mental retardation, emotional disability, learning disability, cerebral palsy, autism, epilepsy, spina bifida, and paraplegia) are in jobs such as baker, bakery counter clerk, customer service clerk, florist, deli clerk, stock clerk, prepared foods clerk, cashier, maintenance, lot attendant, meat cutter, meat wrapper, video clerk, produce clerk, stock clerk, point of sales clerk, playroom attendant, office clerk, and human resource manager. The philosophy of "ability, not disability" means that arbitrary limitations are not placed on employees with disabilities.

CREATE ORGANIZATIONAL STRUCTURES TO SUPPORT THE CHANGE EFFORT

In the early stages of change, some organizations use a task force to determine how to integrate PWDs into the organization. A task force can include representatives from different parts of an organization and help obtain commitment to solutions that are identified. Another structural approach used by organizations (e.g., SunTrust Bank) is a diversity council. At SunTrust Bank, top managers are assigned to diversity initiatives (such as increasing the employment of PWDs) that are aligned with business strategies. These managers must periodically report the progress and achievements of their initiatives. SunTrust Bank also established a Disability Resource Center—a central clearinghouse for information dissemination regarding PWDs. Similarly, Hewlett-Packard has an Accessibility Program Office which serves as a central location for coordinating disability issues.

FOCUS HUMAN RESOURCE PROGRAMS AND PRACTICES ON HIRING AND RETAINING PWDS

The companies profiled in this book use an array of programs and practices to increase the employment of PWDs. Some programs are novel and innovative while others are more traditional strategies for handling employment issues. Since there is little to no research on the effectiveness of these various programs and practices for hiring and retaining PWDs, what will be described next may be thought of as a menu of choices that organizations might use depending upon their particular circumstances. It is probably best to select programs that you believe will fit your organization, try them out, collect data, and see if they work. For programs that prove effective, keep on using them. For programs that don't produce results, discontinue them and go back to the drawing board to try other programs.

Recruit PWDs early. Many of the companies in this book (e.g., Microsoft and Giant Eagle) believe that one of the best ways to increase the employment of PWDs is to recruit them early—while they are still in school. Cooperative ventures with schools and universities, such as internships and mentoring programs, provide companies the opportunity to identify the most talented PWDs early on and perhaps have them committed to full-time employment upon graduation. Internship programs also serve as job tryouts and allow both the company and the PWD to determine if the job is a good fit. Mentoring programs, especially those involving PWDs from the company as mentors would seem to be especially effective at helping prepare young PWDs for their future careers.

Use community-based organizations for sourcing and training. All of the companies in this book—from the small A&F Wood Products to the large Microsoft—use community-based nonprofit organizations for either sourcing applicants with disabilities or for providing training about PWDs. Giant Eagle uses community-based organizations to provide training to their human resource managers. Staff from the community-based organizations actually deliver the training. For them, the community-based organizations serve as quasi-training departments that specialize in PWD issues. Giant Eagle also uses community-based organizations as quasi-external employee/affinity groups for their employees with disabilities. In this capacity, the community-based organizations serve as support groups for store employees with disabilities. Since each Giant Eagle store has only a small number of employees with disabilities, creating more formal employee/affinity groups is not feasible.

Match jobs to PWDs. Many of the companies in this book, such as Giant Eagle, are adamant about simultaneously not limiting the jobs that PWDs might obtain and yet not lowering their qualifications for hiring. They embrace the hiring philosophy of focusing on ability and not disability. Preconceived notions of what jobs PWDs can and cannot do are replaced with creative solutions for adapting jobs to PWDs. Their success in placing PWDs in virtually all jobs in the organization is a testament to their efforts—they walk the talk. However, they also place heavy emphasis on matching the skills and interests of the PWD with the available jobs. Matching PWDs to jobs they can perform increases the probability of a successful outcome for both the employee and the company.

Train recruiters, coworkers, and PWDs. All of the companies in this book use one or more type of training to move their managers and employees to become receptive to hiring and working with PWDs. Recruiter training is common at companies such as Microsoft and SunTrust Bank. This type of training typically addresses such issues as how to adapt interview questions to individuals with specific types of disabilities. Coworkers of employees with disabilities also are provided training at companies such as Microsoft and Hewlett-Packard. This type of training typically addresses such issues as how to behave and how to communicate with individuals who have specific types of disabilities. This type of training includes both general disability awareness content (providing general information about PWDs) as well as specific disability content—sensitizing and preparing coworkers (e.g., teaching sign language) for the introduction of a person with a particular disability (e.g., deafness) into their work group or unit. PWDs themselves also receive training at many companies, from Microsoft and Hewlett-Packard to Giant Eagle and A&F Wood Products. This training ranges from on-the-job training to job coaches to mentors, and frequently focuses on helping PWDs make the transition from school to work.

Approach reasonable job accommodations systematically. Many of the companies in this book (e.g. Microsoft and SunTrust Bank) have created a centralized budget for reasonable accommodations in the company. That is, any necessary funding for reasonable accommodations comes from a corporate account and not a unit or department account. The rationale for doing so is to remove any disincentive a hiring manager might have about hiring a PWD because of the cost of accommodations. Microsoft has an ADA Accommodations Committee to coordinate accommodations throughout the company. Marriott enlists community-based organizations to find less costly, but equally effective, job accommodations. They also encourage managers to think creatively about accommodations. A&F Wood Products' supervisors do think creatively about job accommodations (e.g., the supervisor who closed his eyes to imagine what it would take to help a blind employee use power saws). Marriott also has managers explain accommodations to the coworkers of an employee with disabilities. This often overlooked aspect of the accommodation process is important for reducing jealousies and increasing understanding of coworkers about their colleagues with disabilities.

Create affinity (or support) groups for employees with disabilities. Many of the large companies (e.g. Microsoft, Dow, and Hewlett-Packard) in this book create affinity groups for their employees with disabilities. Affinity groups can serve a number of purposes for PWDs: (a) provide social and emotional support, (b) raise issues of importance, and (c) share information. Dow provides their affinity groups with a budget and assigns a senior executive to sponsor the group. They also use their affinity group as a research laboratory. By observing the group, they learn how to improve human resource practices and policies that affect their employees with disabilities. Hewlett-Packard expands the boundaries of their affinity groups for PWDs by including friends and relatives. And, while Giant Eagle doesn't have corporate affinity groups (since there are not enough employees with disabilities in each of their stores to justify having the groups), they do work with community-based organizations to provide similar types of supportive services for their employees. Whatever form they take, affinity groups are an important means for integrating PWDs into an organization.

Examine other human resource practices that can facilitate inclusion of PWDs. Thinking from a systems perspective leads many companies to examine other ways to make changes that improve the employment of PWDs. For example, Giant Eagle realized that to accommodate employees with disabilities, they would need the flexibility to adjust job assignments. They asked for and received union cooperation in providing the flexibility needed. SunTrust Bank realized that another way they could improve the employment of PWDs was to give preference to contractors and vendors that were either owned and operated by PWDs or employed PWDs. A&F Wood

Products adapts work schedules to public transportation schedules, since many of their employees with disabilities do not drive their own vehicles. In many cases, minor changes can amplify the opportunities for PWDs to work at companies like those in this book—all it takes is a little imagination and creativity.

REFREEZING

After the changes have been successfully implemented, the final stage of the organizational change process is refreezing. Refreezing is the stage when an organization locks the new changes into place and ensures that organizational members will adopt the new changes as part of their everyday lives and operations. Typically, organizations in this stage of the change process establish policies, create procedures, and codify changes in such instruments as job descriptions and reward practices. The companies in this book illustrate several strategies for ensuring that the changes will last.

The following represent the range of strategies they use.

Sustain top management support. It is not enough for top management to provide support for efforts to improve the employment of PWDs only at the beginning of the change. Much like with booster shots that continue the benefits of disease protection over time, organizations too need booster shots from their top management to demonstrate that the change is real and permanent. All of the companies profiled in this book have top managers that reinforce their commitment to hiring and retaining PWDs. And, importantly, when top leadership changes (e.g., at Hewlett-Packard), that commitment to PWDs is transferred to their successors. The continuous top management support makes it clear that hiring PWDs is an important business imperative and not a passing fad.

Use early successes in hiring PWDs to lower obstacles and encourage receptivity. Organizational scholar Karl Weick has written that the way to create large-scale organizational change is to begin with small wins—those incremental successes that when accumulated over time result in large impacts.[10] While many of the companies in this book use this approach, none better exemplify it than A&F Wood Products. This small company began by hiring one PWD and helping that person become a successful employee. This led to hiring additional PWDs over time, each one becoming a successful employee. As momentum has built up over time, both management and coworkers have come to realize the benefits of these valuable employees. Today, 35% of their workforce consists of PWDs.

Regularly report progress toward hiring and retaining PWDs. What gets measured gets done is a management aphorism that has some truth behind it. Efforts to increase the hiring and retention of PWDs can become mere window dressing if progress is not measured over time. SunTrust Banks recognizes this and both assigns top executives to its efforts to increase the employment of PWDs, and regularly reports its progress in those efforts. While it is difficult to accurately count the number of PWDs in an organization since it must be voluntarily disclosed by the individual, companies can create an environment where such disclosure is not perceived as an employment threat. Dow Chemical uses an innovative approach to obtain information about their progress in hiring and retaining PWDs—they use exit interviews.

Incorporate PWD awareness in orientation and socialization programs. Since organizations are not static entities, there is a constant flow of people into and out of them, requiring that change be socialized into each new cohort group of employees. To ensure that new employees are socialized about disability issues, companies can follow the example of Microsoft and incorporate these issues into their orientation programs. Orientation programs can be used to ensure all new employees understand management's values about hiring PWDs as well as encouraging PWDs to seek assistance in such endeavors as obtaining reasonable accommodations.

Create a supportive work environment. A supportive work environment is one in which PWDs—and for that matter all employees—are provided with the tools, guidance, resources, and so on to help them succeed. Creating a supportive work environment starts with the supervisor or manager who can both lead by example and provide encouragement and assistance for all employees—including PWDs. This is exemplified in the anecdote described earlier where one supervisor at A&F Wood Products taught an employee with a disability how to drive on icy roads after work to enable the employee to get to work on time. Another supervisor at A&F Wood Products helped redesign a job involving power saws so that a blind employee could perform it. The ultimate criterion of success for creating a supportive work environment is when you observe coworkers helping coworkers and everyone working toward shared goals.

For global companies, create action plans for each country. Dow takes a global perspective on hiring PWDs. While they meet the more demanding expectations of some countries to hire PWDs because it is required, they nevertheless make efforts to increase their hiring of PWDs at all of their global locations. Hewlett-Packard requires a country action plan from each of its global operations. This provides each unit the opportunity to tailor its plan for hiring PWDs to the circumstances of the particular location.

Publicize accomplishments internally and externally. Six of the companies profiled in this book completed the nomination process and received awards for hiring PWDs from the U.S. Department of Labor (the New Freedom Initiative Awards). By taking this step, each of these companies demonstrated that they were both proud of their accomplishments and that they value PWDs as employees. By taking actions to receive public recognition, companies reinforce the message that PWDs are valued as employees and that their organizations are open and receptive to hiring and retaining them. Furthermore, by publicizing these accomplishments internally, managers and employees get the message that hiring and retaining PWDs is an important management value—one that they must adhere to if they want to be successful in the company.

Creating a Disability-Friendly Culture
Unfreezing

1. Determine what needs to change.
   - Change attitudes.
   - Change behaviors.
2. Ensure that there is strong support from upper management.
   - Issue top management directives.
   - Assign executives to lead the change.
   - Emphasize the business case for hiring PWDs.
3. Create the need for change.
   - Open up new markets of consumers with disabilities.
   - Align PWD initiative with business strategy.
4. Understand and address the doubts and concerns of managers and employees.
   - Emphasize that hiring standards will not be lowered.
   - Ask how they would want to be treated if they became disabled.

Moving

1. Use top-down and bottom-up change initiatives.
   - Emphasize the business case from the top.
   - Demonstrate the business case from the bottom.

2. Develop a disability philosophy.
   - Focus on ability, not disability.
   - Accommodations, access, and attitudes.
3. Create organizational structures to support the change effort.
   - Use task forces with members from different parts of the organization.
   - Assign top managers to change initiatives.
   - Create a central information clearinghouse for disability issues.
4. Focus human resource practices on hiring and retaining PWDs.
   - Recruit PWDs early—while they are still in school.
   - Use community-based organizations for sourcing and training.
   - Match jobs to PWDs.
   - Train recruiters, coworkers, and PWDs.
   - Approach reasonable job accommodations systematically.
   - Create affinity (or support) groups for employees with disabilities.
   - Examine other human resource practices that can facilitate inclusion of PWDs, such as adapting work schedules, outsourcing to vendors that hire PWDs, etc.

Refreezing

1. Sustain top management support.
   - Periodically reaffirm commitment to hiring PWDs.
   - Participate in disability events, such as making a speech.
2. Use early successes in hiring PWDs to lower obstacles and encourage receptivity
   - Start small—one person or one unit.
   - Publicize success stories and achievements of PWDs.
3. Regularly report progress toward hiring and retaining PWDs.
   - Measure progress in hiring and retaining PWDs regularly.
   - Use exit interviews to obtain information about PWDs.
4. Incorporate PWD awareness in orientation and socialization programs.
   - Use orientation to provide new employees with disability awareness.
   - Use orientation to encourage PWDs to obtain reasonable accommodations.

5. Create a supportive work environment.

   - Provide tools, guidance, and resources for PWDs to succeed.

   - Encourage supervisors to take a leadership role.

6. For global companies, create action plans for each country.

   - Tailor programs to hire and retain PWDs to local cultures.

   - Identify and meet the most stringent standards.

7. Publicize accomplishments internally and externally.

   - Self-nominate for recognition, such as the New Freedom Initiative Award.

   - Use newsletters and other internal communication media to publicize accomplishments of employees with disabilities.

CONCLUSION

Diversity efforts, such as improving the employment of PWDs, often fail for several reasons.[11] One, they fail when companies start them because they are the latest fad or because an outside consultant or agency recommends they do so. Diversity programs to improve the employment of PWDs typically have not been fads; quite the contrary, it usually takes more convincing to persuade managers and employees of the need to undertake them. Furthermore, the companies in this book began their efforts to hire and retain more PWDs primarily for bottom-line business reasons, not because of external pressures. Two, diversity efforts fail when they are not tailored or customized to fit the particular organization. While the companies in this book have some common elements in their efforts to hire and retain PWDs, each one creates a unique blend that fits their own circumstances. And finally, diversity efforts fail when they only provide awareness training and do not establish policies and procedures to ensure that behaviors change too. While awareness training is important—and many of the companies in this book provide it to their employees—these companies also go further in ensuring that more than just attitudes are changed.

While there is no one best way to implement a change effort to improve the employment of PWDs, there are some good alternatives as illustrated by the companies in this book. Two major conclusions can be drawn from this discussion. One, taking a systems view of change helps organizations consider how different elements interact and reinforce one another in moving employees toward a desired state. In this case that desired state is greater receptivity

toward hiring and working with PWDs—focusing on their abilities and not their disabilities. Two, organizational change is a process that takes place in stages over time. To undertake a change effort to improve the employment of PWDs is to sign on for a long-term involvement. Even the best companies, such as those profiled in this book, have made incremental improvements in their hiring and retention of PWDs. It will take some time before PWDs are truly integrated into corporate workforces.

CHAPTER 12

Conclusion

Mark L. Lengnick-Hall

Hiring and retaining people with disabilities is a win–win–win solution to a number of problems. First, many people with disabilities want to work but currently are unemployed. They want to work for the same reasons that nondisabled people want to work: to obtain income, to support themselves and their families, to get the satisfaction that can be derived from a job and a career, and to make contributions to organizations and society. Second, employers need the best talent available to compete effectively in a global economy. Capitalizing on a source of good employees could make the difference between success and failure in the marketplace. And third, society is better off when more people with disabilities are able to find productive work. People with disabilities then pay taxes, have more income to purchase goods and services, and reduce their dependency on taxpayer-supported assistance programs. If hiring and retaining people with disabilities truly is a win–win–win solution, why isn't it happening to a greater extent than it is now?

In the first section of this book, we tried to answer that question. Our conclusion is that there are a number of factors contributing to why more people with disabilities are not employed. Making organizations more accessible to people with disabilities is a recent phenomenon resulting largely from the passage of the Americans with Disabilities Act (ADA) in 1990. Prior to that, most organizations designed buildings, facilities, operations, and jobs around the model employee—someone who had no disabilities. While much progress has been made since the passage of the ADA, much is still needed to create workplaces that are truly inclusive. Attitudes are another big factor in explaining why more people with disabilities are not employed. Many managers and employees hold ambivalent attitudes about people with disabilities. While they admire people with disabilities who overcome obstacles and achieve difficult goals, these same managers and employees believe that people with disabilities either cannot do many jobs or that the costs of accommodating them are so great that it does not make good business sense to hire them. And, while social assistance programs do much good in supporting people with disabilities in their daily lives, unfortunately they also create some disincentives to employment because of the way they are structured. For these and other reasons, fewer people with disabilities who are qualified and want to work are employed compared to their nondisabled counterparts. If this is the case, how do we move toward the win–win–win solution?

In the second section of the book, we described how leading companies have set an example on how to hire, retain, and benefit from people with disabilities. These companies are unique because they embrace the value of people with disabilities as employees and seek them out. They go beyond merely complying with the law. These companies are unique because they develop programs, practices, and policies that create a disability-friendly culture—an inclusive culture that welcomes people with disabilities because of what they can bring to the workplace. These companies are unique because they believe that any incremental costs incurred to accommodate people with disabilities are more than offset by the benefits obtained. It is sound business decision making.

Both large and small companies and companies in different industries have discovered how to hire and retain people with disabilities. The large companies profiled in this book have many resources and formal programs they bring to the problem of increasing the employment of people with disabilities. Executive task forces, diversity councils, affinity groups, and other methods demonstrate both the seriousness of their efforts and provide the means to accomplishing their goals. However, even small companies, like A&F Wood Products (profiled in this book) can be equally effective without all of the firepower. By partnering with local community agencies and taking a pragmatic approach to job accommodations, A&F Wood Products has been able to meet their needs for labor and at the same time provide meaningful work for people with disabilities. So, size matters in terms of resources that can be brought to bear upon the problem, but when it comes to effectiveness, even the smallest of companies can achieve success.

In the third section of the book, we have synthesized what we learned about hiring and retaining people with disabilities and provided guidelines companies can follow. One thing is clear from studying the companies profiled in this book: they hire people with disabilities because it is a good business decision. All of these companies have concluded that hiring people with disabilities can help them become more profitable and competitive in the marketplace. In

Chapter 11, we compiled arguments supporting the business case for hiring people with disabilities. Since many managers and employees need convincing that hiring and retaining people with disabilities is a good idea, we have assembled some of the best reasons that can be used to support that assertion. Ignorance and misinformation about people with disabilities is commonplace and can only be countered by education and factual information. Building a business case for hiring people with disabilities is a starting point for changing people's attitudes.

While education and providing factual information is important to improving the employment of people with disabilities, it is not enough to create organizational change by itself. In Chapter 12, we presented a three-stage model of organizational change to help employers plan a systematic effort to become more disability-friendly. For each stage of the model of organizational change, we illustrated how the companies in this book have developed their own action plans. No two companies in the book approached their organizational change efforts to employ more people with disabilities in the same way. While there are some common features, such as affinity groups used by several companies, each company tailored its own approach to fit its own particular circumstances. Consequently, while we present a model of organizational change as a guide for employers, we encourage employers to adapt it to their own environments.

Where does change begin? It can begin at the top. Certainly companies like Microsoft and CEO Bill Gates demonstrate that mandates from executives can trigger change at lower levels. Managers and employees follow directives from the top because to do otherwise might jeopardize their jobs. Complying with directives from the top may also be seen as a way to obtain favorable evaluations and advance careers. Managers and employees who are asked to hire and work with people with disabilities may be reluctant to do so without admonition from above. However, once they do hire and work with people with disabilities, their attitudes and behaviors are likely to change as they discover that many of their negative stereotypes and beliefs are wrong and that in fact people with disabilities make good employees.

Demonstrating the benefits of hiring people with disabilities in a field office or lower down the organizational hierarchy is another starting point for effectuating change. As SunTrust Banks demonstrated, pilot projects begun at local field offices sparked interest and enthusiasm that spread throughout the company. Managers want to emulate the success of their colleagues and thus seek out what they are doing to achieve it. When hiring and retaining people with disabilities can be shown to improve the bottom line by increasing revenues, decreasing costs, or both, most managers will jump at the opportunity to get on the bandwagon.

Improving the employment of people with disabilities is no easy task nor will it be achieved quickly. Even the best companies, like those profiled in this book, discover that creating the kind of needed organizational change takes time, resources, and persistence. One difficult challenge is sustaining efforts across changes in management. To be effective, hiring and retaining people with disabilities must be viewed as a business necessity or a business value, and not as a passing fad.

Good ideas spread quickly in this age of information technology. We hope that the good ideas outlined in this book will be picked up by companies, implemented, and shared with others. As more and more companies discover the hidden talent of people with disabilities, we hope that someday soon we will no longer be able to use the word *hidden* when talking about talented people with disabilities.

APPENDIX 1

Tax Incentives for Hiring People with Disabilities

Robert R. Hull

ARCHITECTURAL/TRANSPORTATION TAX DEDUCTION (ATTD)

All (for-profit) businesses are eligible. Businesses may take an annual deduction of up to $15,000 a year for expenses incurred to remove barriers for people with disabilities for amounts in excess of the $15,000 maximum. Amounts in excess of the $15,000 annual deduction may be depreciated.

DISABLED ACCESS CREDIT (DAC)

Small (for-profit) businesses that in the previous year earned a maximum of $1 million in revenue or had 30 or fewer full-time employees are eligible. Small businesses can receive a tax credit to provide Americans with Disabilities Act (ADA) accommodations to employees with disabilities. The credit is 50 percent of expenditures that are more than $250, not to exceed $10,250, for a maximum benefit of $5,000.

MENTOR–PROTÉGÉ PROGRAM (MPP)

For-profit businesses that employ people with severe disabilities (as defined by Section 8064A of Public Law 102-172) and subcontract work from a prime contractor to the U.S. Department of Defense are eligible. This program provides dollar-for-dollar reimbursement of costs up to 10 percent of the total contract value for protégé, or credit, whereby the mentor receives from two to four times the cost of assistance provided to the protege in credits toward the mentor's Small Disadvantaged Business subcontracting goals.

SOCIAL SECURITY ADMINISTRATION EMPLOYMENT NETWORK CASH PROVISIONS (SSAENCP)

All businesses (except 501(c)4 lobbying organizations) are eligible. Employees who are receiving social security benefits must obtain or advance in employment to the extent that they no longer receive Social Security Administration benefits. The Employment Network receives a monthly cash reimbursement of 40 percent of the average national monthly Social Security Disability Insurance (SSDI) or Social Security Insurance (SSI) benefit payments. So long as the individual is employed at this salary or wage level, the Employment Network receives the cash payment, which could continue for as long as 60 months.

VETERANS JOB TRAINING PROGRAM

Employers (for-profit and nonprofit) can receive reimbursement up to 50 percent of a veteran's salary and the Veterans Administration can supplement a training wage. Employers then pay payroll taxes based only on their pay to the veteran. Needed tools and equipment are supplied by VA. Veterans with service-connected disabilities who face employment barriers are eligible.

WORK OPPORTUNITY TAX CREDIT (WOTC)

All for-profit firms are eligible. Employees must be from one of nine groups, including people with disabilities and veterans with service-connected disabilities completing a state vocational rehabilitation or Veterans Administration vocational rehabilitation program. Tax credit of up to $2,400.

WELFARE-TO-WORK TAX CREDIT (WtW)

All for-profit firms are eligible. Employees must be part of a family that has received Temporary Assistance to Needy Families (TANF) or Aid to Families with Dependent Children (AFDC). Tax credit of up to $8,500.

Architectural/Transportation Tax Deduction (ATTD)

Eligible Users	All businesses
Description	Businesses may take an annual deduction for expenses incurred to remove physical, structural, and transportation barriers for people with disabilities (or the elderly) at the workplace.
Incentives	Businesses may take a tax deduction of up to $15,000 a year for expenses incurred to remove barriers for people with disabilities. Amounts in excess of the $15,000 maximum annual deduction may be depreciated.
Covered Expenses	This can be used for a variety of costs to make a facility or public transportation vehicle, owned or leased for use in the business, more accessible to and usable by people with disabilities. Examples include the cost of: <ul><li>Providing accessible parking spaces, ramps, and curb cuts;</li><li>Providing telephones, water fountains, and restrooms which are accessible to people using wheelchairs;</li><li>Making walkways at least 48 inches wide.</li></ul>
Expenses Not Covered	The deduction may not be used for expenses incurred for new construction, or for a complete renovation of a facility or public transportation vehicle, or for the normal replacement of depreciable property.
Procedures	The amount spent is subtracted from the total income of a business to establish its taxable income. In order for expenses to be deductible, accessibility standards established under the Section 190 regulations must be met.

Deadlines: None (can be used every year).
Forms: None.
Legislation: IRS Code Section 190, Barrier Removal.
Note: Small businesses may use both DAC and ADDT together, if the expenses incurred qualify under both Sections 44 and 190. For example, if a business spent $12,000 for access adaptations, it would qualify for a $5,000 tax credit and a $7,000 tax deduction.

Disabled Access Credit (DAC)

Eligible Users	Small businesses that in the previous year earned a maximum of $1 million in revenue or had 30 or fewer full-time employees
Description	Eligible small businesses can receive a tax credit for paying or incurring expenses to provide access to people with disabilities (these expenses must be for compliance with the Americans with Disabilities Act of 1990).
Incentives	The credit is 50 percent of expenditures over $250, not to exceed $10,250, for a maximum benefit of $5,000. The credit amount is subtracted from the total tax liability after calculating taxes.
Covered Expenses	Examples include: • Sign language interpreters for employees or customers who have hearing impairments • Readers for employees or customers who have visual impairments • The purchase of adaptive equipment or the modification of equipment • The production of print materials in alternate formats (e.g., braille, audiotape, large print) • The removal of architectural barriers in buildings or vehicles
Expenses Not Covered	The tax credit does not apply to the costs of new construction, and a building being modified must have been placed in service before November 5, 1990.
Procedures	Complete the one-page IRS Form 8826 along with regular business tax forms, to be filed for the calendar year in which expenditures were incurred.

Deadlines: None (can be used every year).
Forms: IRS Form 8826.
Legislation: IRS Code Section 144.
Note: Small businesses may use both DAC and ADDT together, if the expenses incurred qualify under both Sections 44 and 190. For example, if a business spent $12,000 for access adaptations, it would qualify for a $5,000 tax credit and a $7,000 tax deduction.

Mentor-Protégé Program

Eligible Users	**Mentor**—must have at least one active subcontracting plan and be eligible for federal contracts **Protégé**—A qualified organization employing people with severe disabilities as defined in Section 8064A of Public Law 102-172
Description	Businesses that employ people with severe disabilities (as defined above) and subcontract work from a prime contactor to the U.S. Dept. of Defense may receive technical assistance in areas such as production, management, financing, etc. The prime contractor (the mentor) is reimbursed by the federal agency for the costs of the technical assistance provided to the protégé.
Incentives	**Reimbursement of Costs**, dollar for dollar, both direct and indirect for mentor, and up to 10% of total contract value for protégé, *or* **Credit**, whereby the mentor receives from two to four times the cost of assistance provided to the protégé in credits toward the mentor's SDB subcontracting goals (as required for contracts over $500K, or $1 million for construction).

Reimbursable Costs	Types of Credit Available
For the mentor: Direct Costs: providing developmental assistance with the mentor's personnel. **Indirect Costs:** Travel and subsistence, incidental supplies and materials. **For the protégé:** Costs not specifically addressed in the legislation, which are otherwise considered allowable, allocable and reasonable. These primarily include travel and subsistence, and incidental supplies and materials.	1. Credit for any reasonable and allowable costs incurred by the mentor that were not reimbursed under the mentor's cooperative agreement or as a separately priced contract line item 2. Credit for developmental assistance costs that have been reimbursed via inclusion in indirect expense pools 3. Credit for developmental assistance costs not eligible for reimbursement (to the degree that such costs were identified in the original mentor–protégé agreement) 4. Credit for all developmental costs where the mentor–protégé agreement is for credit only

(continued)

123

Mentor-Protégé Program (*continued*)

Procedures	1. The first act of participation for either party, Mentor or Protégé, is to find a counterpart. 2. Once a suitable partner is located the requirements of the Program must be met (see Eligible Users). 3. When these requirements have been met the mentor must complete the Mentor Application (see below in Forms), that is if they are not already a mentor, and submit it prior to the agreement. 4. Upon submitting the Mentor Application the two parties should commence talks discerning what both hope to accomplish through the agreement, setting goals for themselves. 5. Next, both parties submit the Mentor–Protégé Agreement Application (see below in Forms). 6. In addition, in accordance with DFARS Appendix I-111, both a mentor and protégé firm must report on the progress made under active mentor–protégé agreements semiannually and the protégé firm must report on the progress made under the Mentor–Protégé Agreement annually. The protégé firm is also required to provide data on the firm for 2 fiscal years after the expiration of the Program participation term (see below in Forms).

Deadlines: None–program is ongoing; however, different types of contracts can require internal deadlines.
Forms[1]: Mentor Agreement Template, Protégé Agreement Template, Semi-Annual Report,
[1] Mentors applying for Reimbursement of Costs must apply directly through the service/agency, as each might have differences in data required, application process, and timing of application.
Legislation: Public Law 101-510, enacted 1990.

Social Security Administration (SSA) Employment Network Cash Provisions

Eligible Users	All business entities, for-profit and not-for-profit (other than 501(c)4 lobbying organizations) that are not disbarred from federal grants and contracts.
Description	An Employment Network (EN) can consist of individual business entities or consortia of business entities or organizations. Business entities or organizations may participate in more than one EN. The EN provides services to individuals with disabilities who receive Social Security benefits to enable them to obtain or advance in employment to the extent that they no longer receive SSA benefits (SSDI or SSI; Medicaid/Medicare may continue).
Incentives	Once the Ticket-holder (beneficiary) achieves "substantial gainful activity" ($800/month in 2003 and $810 a month in 2004), the EN receives a monthly cash reimbursement of 40% of the average national monthly SSDI or SSI benefit payments. So long as the individual is employed at this salary or wage level the EN receives the cash payment. This may continue up to 60 months.
Current Payments	Monthly cash reimbursements beginning in 2003 to an Employment Network (for a former SSDI beneficiary) can total $19,680 over the 60 months of Ticket eligibility. Monthly cash reimbursements beginning in 2003 to an Employment Network (for a former SSI beneficiary) can total $11,760 over the 60 months of Ticket eligibility. Monthly cash reimbursements for dual beneficiaries (former recipients of both SSDI and SSI) will be paid at the SSDI rate.
Procedures	1. Tickets-to-Work are being mailed to SSA beneficiaries on a phased schedule over three years (2001–2004). Once a beneficiary's state of residence begins participation in the program, he or she can request or will eventually receive a Ticket.
	2. The Ticket holder may then select an approved Employment Network and "assign" his or her ticket to that EN.
	3. The beneficiary and the EN then agree upon an Individual Work Plan, which details the services that the EN will provide to that beneficiary in return for assignment of the Ticket.
	4. The Individual Work Plan must be approved by Maximus, Inc., the Program Manager for the Social Security Administration.

(continued)

5. The beneficiary receives services such as training and employment preparation, and then obtains employment. The EN continues to provide employment support for the 60 months of the Ticket eligibility.
6. When the beneficiary's Social Security benefits cease due to his or her earned income, the Employment Network files for the monthly cash reimbursement.
7. If the EN is a consortium, and more than one business entity or organization has provided services, the monthly cash reimbursement may be divided between them as they agree.

Deadlines: None–program is ongoing; however, different types of contracts can require internal deadlines.

Forms: Approved application as an Employment Network (EN); Individual Work Plans for Ticket Users; Annual Reports.

Legislation: Ticket to Work and Work Incentives Improvement Act, Public Law 106-170, enacted 1999.

Note: General source information: Social Security Administration: http://www.ssa.gov/work; Maximus, Inc. (Program Manager) http://www.yourtickettowork.com; or toll-free telephone number: 1-866-968-7842 (Voice); or toll-free telephone number: 1-866-833-2967 (TDD)

Work Opportunity Tax Credit (WOTC)

Eligible Users	Not-for-profit firms ineligible. All for-profit firms, regardless of size, are eligible.
Eligible Employees	People with disabilities who completed or are completing rehabilitative services from a State or the U.S. Department of Veterans Affairs.
Incentives	Tax credit of up to $2,400 for each new hire: 40% of qualified first-year wages for those who are employed 400 or more hours, 25% of those who are employed 120 hours.
Restrictions	1. Qualified capped at $6,000 per employee. WOTC applies only to new employees hired after September 30, 1996, and before January 1, 2004. (Note: Employers have a maximum combined period of two years to claim WOTC or WtW. Employers cannot claim both on the same individual in the same taxable year.)
	2. Credits cannot be claimed for wages paid to relatives.
	3. No tax credit can be claimed for federally subsidized on-the-job training. However, wages paid after the subsidy expires can qualify for tax credit.
	4. Any individual who previously worked for the employer and does not meet the definition of "qualifying re-hire" is ineligible.
Procedures	1. Complete the one-page IRS Form 8850 by the day the job offer is made.
	2. Complete either the one-page ETA Form 9061 or Form 9062:
	a. If the new employee has already been conditionally certified as belonging to a WOTC target group, complete the bottom part of ETA Form 9062 (and sign and date it), that he or she has been given by a State Employment Security Agency or participating agency, e.g., a Job Corps center.
	b. If the new employee has not been conditionally certified, the employer and/or the new employee must fill out and complete, sign, and date ETA Form 9061
	3. Mail the signed IRS and ETA forms to the employer's State Employment Security Agency. The IRS form must be mailed within 21 days of the employee's employment start date.

Deadlines: The Work Opportunity Tax Credit is in force until December 31, 2003 (program subject to yearly Congressional renewal).
Forms: IRS Form 8850; ETA Form 9061, or Form 9062.
Legislation: Small Business Job Protection Act of 1996 (P.L. 104-188).

Welfare-to-Work Tax Credit (WtW)

Eligible Users	All for-profit firms, regardless of size, are eligible. Not-for-profit firms ineligible.
Eligible Employees	Individuals who have been certified by the "designated local agency" as a member of a family that received Temporary Assistance to Needy Families (TANF) or Aid to Families with Dependent Children (AFDC).
Incentives	Tax credit of up to $8,500 for each new hire: 35% of qualified first-year wages, 50% of qualified second-year wages. Employees must be employed at least 400 hours or 180 days.
Restrictions	1. Qualified wages (which include tax-exempt amounts received under accident and health plans as well as educational and dependent assistance programs) capped at $10,000 per employee. WtW applies only to new employees hired after December 31, 1997, and before January 1, 2004. (Note: Employers have a maximum combined period of two years to claim WOTC credit or WtW. Employers cannot claim both on the same individual in the same taxable year.)
	2. Credits cannot be claimed for wages paid to relatives.
	3. No tax credit can be claimed for federally subsidized on-the-job training. However, wages paid after the subsidy expires can qualify for tax credit.
	4. Any individual who previously worked for the employer and does not meet the definition of "qualifying re-hire" is ineligible.
Procedures	1. Complete the one-page IRS Form 8850 by the day the job offer is made.
	2. Complete either the one-page ETA Form 9061 or Form 9062:
	a. If the new employee has already been conditionally certified as belonging to a WOTC target group, complete the bottom part of ETA Form 9062 (and sign and date it), that he or she has been given by a State Employment Security Agency or participating agency, e.g., a Job Corps center.
	b. If the new employee has not been conditionally certified, the employer and/or the new employee must fill out and complete, sign and date ETA Form 9061.
	3. Mail the signed IRS and ETA forms to the employer's State Employment Security Agency. The IRS form must be mailed within 21 days of the employee's employment start date.

Deadlines: The Welfare-to-Work Tax Incentive is in force until December 31, 2003 (program subject to yearly Congressional renewal).
Forms: IRS Form 8850; ETA Form 9061 or 9062.
Legislation: Taxpayer Relief Act of 1997.

APPENDIX 2

Resources for Hiring People with Disabilities

Robert R. Hull

FEDERAL GOVERNMENT

INTERAGENCY

Disability.gov

This site provides a collection of resources, services, and information available from the federal government.
www.disability.gov

ABLEDATA

ABLEDATA provides a database of more than 20,000 assistive devices ranging from eating utensils to wheelchairs.
www.abledata.com

Coordinating Council on Emergency Preparedness and Individuals with Disabilities

This group provides a framework of emergency preparedness guidelines for federal agencies. Many are adaptable to businesses.
www.dhs.gov/disabilitypreparedness/resourcecenter

Access Board

An independent federal agency, the Access Board sets policies, regulations and standards for all forms of access and accommodations for individuals with disabilities.
www.access-board.gov

National Council on Disability

Periodically commissions national polling organizations to conduct surveys of people with disabilities concerning topics such as employment.
www.ncd.gov

Office of Personnel Management

Handles employment of individuals with disabilities within the federal government.
www.opm.gov

DEPARTMENT OF LABOR

The Employment and Training Administration

Designed to direct adults, youth, dislocated workers, and workforce professionals through the training of the workforce and the placement of workers in jobs through employment services. Periodically funds disability and employment training grants.
www.doleta.gov

Office of Disability Employment Policy (ODEP)

Coordinates disability employment policies as they interact with other labor and workforce programs.
www.dol.gov/odep

Employer Assistance and Recruiting Network (EARN)

The Employer Assistance and Recruiting Network (EARN) assists employers in locating and recruiting qualified workers with disabilities. EARN, which is a service of the Office of Disability Employment Policy, can also provide technical assistance on general disability employment-related issues.

www.dol.gov/odep

Workforce Recruitment Program

The Workforce Recruitment Program database contains profiles of talented college students with disabilities for summer or permanent hiring needs. These candidates, from more than 200 colleges and universities, represent all majors, and range from college freshmen to graduate students and law students.

www.dol.gov/odep

Disabilityinfo.gov

The Office of Disability Employment Policy, Department of Labor hosts this information website.

www.disabilityinfo.gov

DEPARTMENT OF EDUCATION

Rehabilitation Services Administration

RSA sponsors the federal–state network of Vocational Rehabilitation programs, as well as a number of Special Demonstration grant programs.

www.ed.gov/rsa

National Institute for Disability and Rehabilitation Research

NIDRR is one of the largest funders of university and nonprofit research centers in the federal government. The following illustrate NIDRR programs:
Disability and Business Technical Assistance Centers
Rehabilitation Research and Training Centers
Rehabilitation Engineering Research Centers
www.ed.gov/nidrr

Americans with Disabilities Act Technical Assistance Program

An ADA information program available through the nationwide network of Disability and Business Technical Assistance Centers

www.adata.org

Job Accommodation Network

Provides individualized worksite accommodation solutions and provides technical assistance with ADA and other disability-related legislation. Includes the Small Business and Self Employment Service (SBSES).
http://www.jan.wvu.edu/

SOCIAL SECURITY ADMINISTRATION

Social Security Online

The official website of the Social Security Administration includes Blue Book (Disability Evaluation under Social Security); Work Incentives definitions and Encyclopedia; 2001 Redbook on Employment Support.
www.ssa.gov

Social Security Administration

Forms location
http://www.ssa.gov/online

Office of Employment Support Programs

Information for people with disabilities who want to work. This site also hosts a section for Employers.
www.ssa.gov/work

DEPARTMENT OF JUSTICE

Information on compliance with the Americans with Disabilities Act from the Disability Rights Section.
www.usdoj.gov/disabilities

DEPARTMENT OF TRANSPORTATION

Provides a Disability Resource center and a website focused on emergency preparedness in the transportation industry.
www.drc.dot.gov
www.dotcr.ost.dot.gov/asp/emergencyprep.asp

United States Small Business Administration

Information and a startup guide with many supporting resources.
http://www.sba.gov/starting_business/startup/guide.html

Small Business Development Center—National Information Clearinghouse

Provides links to other small business development sites.
http://sbdcnet.utsa.edu

Association of Small Business Development Centers

Information on local resources, training, and loan programs.
www.asbdc-us.org

Business-Sponsored Organizations

Business Leadership Network

The US Business Leadership Network (USBLN) is the national organization that supports development and expansion of BLNs across the country, serving as their collective voice. The USBLN recognizes and promotes best practices in hiring, retaining, and marketing to people with disabilities.
www.usbln.com

National Business and Disability Council

The National Business & Disability Council is the leading resource for employers seeking to integrate people with disabilities into the workplace and companies seeking to reach them in the consumer marketplace.
www.nbdc.com

University-Sponsored Organization

Virginia Commonwealth University

The VCU Business Roundtable is a business forum for identifying and addressing factors that inhibit industries from employing workers with disabilities. The roundtable is chaired by C.T. Hill, Chairman, President and CEO

of SunTrust Bank, Mid-Atlantic. The roundtable discusses ways to enhance the productivity of people with disabilities. The ideas generated address and assist companies with issues concerning hiring workers with disabilities.
www.worksupport.com/projects

National Institute of Disability Management and Research (Canada)

The National Institute of Disability Management and Research (NID-MAR), founded in 1994, is an internationally recognized organization committed to reducing the human, social and economic costs of disability. As an education, training and research organization, NIDMAR's primary focus is the implementation of workplace-based reintegration programs which international research has proven is the most effective way of restoring and maintaining workers' abilities, while reducing the costs of disability for workers, employers, government, and insurance carriers. The National Institute's success is the result of collaborative initiatives undertaken by leaders in labor, business, government, education, insurance, and rehabilitation.
www.nidmar.ca/index.asp

INDIVIDUALS WITH DISABILITIES AS ENTREPRENEURS

Chambers of Commerce for Individuals with Disabilities

National cross-disability consumer volunteer organization that uses business principles to improve the economic status of people with disabilities.
www.chamber4us.org

APPENDIX 3

The Cerebral Palsy Research Foundation

Robert R. Hull

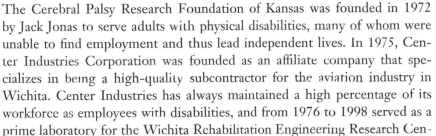

The Cerebral Palsy Research Foundation of Kansas was founded in 1972 by Jack Jonas to serve adults with physical disabilities, many of whom were unable to find employment and thus lead independent lives. In 1975, Center Industries Corporation was founded as an affiliate company that specializes in being a high-quality subcontractor for the aviation industry in Wichita. Center Industries has always maintained a high percentage of its workforce as employees with disabilities, and from 1976 to 1998 served as a prime laboratory for the Wichita Rehabilitation Engineering Research Center. The Wichita RERC was a joint CPRF—Wichita State University College of Engineering project that published many pioneering studies of workplace accommodations.

Today, the mission of CPRF is to provide individuals with disabilities customized services, supports, and technologies, with an emphasis on employment and training, to facilitate their chosen economic and personal independence. The emphasis on employment and training is the special focus of the Division on Employment Services, whose key program is the School of Adaptive Computer Training. Here students with disabilities train at ergonomic computer workstations and graduate with tested certifications as Specialists in all of the Microsoft Office applications—Word, Excel, Access, PowerPoint, Outlook, etc. Employment Services then provides them with placement services, accomplished by establishing a bridge between employer partners in the community and employment candidates to find a long-term, successful match.

With its long tradition of research, the CPRF decided in 1998, as the Rehabilitation Engineering Research Center was closing, to establish a research division that would seek to become an innovative research-and-program development unit, developing new long-term programs to meet the needs of employees with disabilities. In 2000, both an Employment Research and Organizational Development project and the Kansas Benefits Counselors Network were initiated. The development of the research project is described in the Preface. The Kansas Benefits Counselors Network (KBCN) is an innovative approach to the Benefits Planning, Assistance, and Outreach projects created by the Social Security Administration throughout the nation. As the grant funding was insufficient to cover travel throughout the state (Kansas is the 13th largest in the nation), CPRF drew upon communication technology. Volunteer counselors in organizations throughout the state upload and download their customers' documents through a secure, 128-bit encrypted web portal to the benefits specialists at CPRF. Continuing education is provided to these benefits counselors through the Kansas Regents Interactive Television Network (Telenet 2). From a media classroom at Wichita State University, the CPRF benefits specialists provide interactive training with the benefits counselors in one of 11 community college sites near their home community. This minimizes travel costs for everyone.

In March 2002, CPRF opened its Employment Network (EN), accepting Tickets to Work from people receiving Social Security disability benefits and providing them services to obtain or return to work. Again taking an innovative approach, the CPRF Employment Network focuses on strengthening the business community by helping maximize their area recruitment efforts without added expense. Furthermore, by educating employers about the federal tax incentives, the Employment Network contributes to their cost recovery—a win for businesses, and for their employees with disabilities. After the KBCN and EN project concepts had proven themselves over several years, they were relocated in July 2006 from the Research Division to the Division of Employment Services.

Current program development in the Research Division focuses on providing a Volunteers in Tax Assistance (VITA) site and the South Central Kansas Low Income Taxpayers Clinic, funded by the Internal Revenue Service. This clinic provides tax attorney representation free to low income taxpayers who face administrative or tax court controversies with the IRS. CPRF's tax attorney, who is also a qualified Social Security disability benefits specialist, is leading the way toward developing a statewide technical assistance center specializing in the many complex interactions between disability benefits and income taxes as people with disabilities enter the workforce in increasing numbers.

APPENDIX 4

The Americans with Disabilities Act (1990)

Mark L. Lengnick-Hall

From: http://www.eeoc.gov/types/ada.html; http://www.eeoc.gov/facts/adaqa1.html

WHAT IS PROHIBITED?

Title I of the Americans with Disabilities Act of 1990 prohibits private employers, state and local governments, employment agencies and labor unions from discriminating against qualified individuals with disabilities in job application procedures, hiring, firing, advancement, compensation, job training, and other terms, conditions, and privileges of employment.

WHO IS COVERED?

The ADA covers employers with 15 or more employees, including state and local governments. It also applies to employment agencies and to labor organizations. The ADA's nondiscrimination standards also apply to federal sector employees under section 501 of the Rehabilitation Act, as amended, and its implementing rules.

WHAT IS A DISABILITY?

An individual with a disability is a person who

- has a physical or mental impairment that substantially limits one or more major life activities;
- has a record of such an impairment; or
- is regarded as having such an impairment.

WHAT IS A QUALIFIED EMPLOYEE/APPLICANT WITH A DISABILITY?

A qualified employee or applicant with a disability is an individual who, with or without reasonable accommodation, can perform the essential functions of the job in question.

WHAT ARE ESSENTIAL JOB FUNCTIONS?

To be considered a qualified employee/applicant with a disability, a person needs to be able to perform the essential functions of the job. Essential job functions are major, nontrivial tasks required of an employee. This excludes either marginal or incidental tasks. If a written job description has been prepared in advance of advertising or interviewing applicants for a job, this will be considered as evidence, although not necessarily conclusive evidence, of the essential functions of the job.

ARE EMPLOYERS REQUIRED TO GIVE PREFERENTIAL TREATMENT TO APPLICANTS WITH DISABILITIES?

No. An employer is free to select the most qualified applicant available and to make decisions based on reasons unrelated to the existence or consequence of a disability. For example, if two persons apply for a job opening as a typist, one a person with a disability who accurately types 50 words per minute, the other a person without a disability who accurately types 75 words per minute, the employer may hire the applicant with the higher typing speed, if typing speed is needed for successful performance of the job.

ARE EMPLOYERS REQUIRED TO HAVE AN AFFIRMATIVE ACTION PLAN FOR PEOPLE WITH DISABILITIES?

There are no requirements for affirmative action plans. Employers are not required to set goals and timetables for hiring people with disabilities. Employers are not required to keep records of the number of employees with disabilities (in fact this is quite difficult since employers cannot require individuals to disclose their disabilities if they do not wish to).

ARE EMPLOYERS REQUIRED TO HIRE SOMEONE WHO POSES A DIRECT THREAT TO THE HEALTH AND SAFETY OF OTHERS?

No. The ADA expressly permits employers to establish qualification standards that will exclude individuals who pose a direct threat—i.e., a significant risk of substantial harm—to the health or safety of the individual or of others, if that risk cannot be lowered to an acceptable level by reasonable accommodation. However, an employer may not simply assume that a threat exists; the employer must establish through objective, medically supportable methods that there is genuine risk that substantial harm could occur in the workplace. By requiring employers to make individualized judgments based on reliable medical or other objective evidence rather than on generalizations, ignorance, fear, patronizing attitudes, or stereotypes, the ADA recognizes the need to balance the interests of people with disabilities against the legitimate interests of employers in maintaining a safe workplace.

WHAT IS REASONABLE ACCOMMODATION?

Reasonable accommodation may include, but is not limited to

- making existing facilities used by employees readily accessible to and usable by persons with disabilities.
- job restructuring, modifying work schedules, reassignment to a vacant position;
- acquiring or modifying equipment or devices, adjusting or modifying examinations, training materials, or policies, and providing qualified readers or interpreters.

WHEN MUST AN EMPLOYER MAKE REASONABLE ACCOMMODATION?

An employer is required to make a reasonable accommodation to the known disability of a qualified applicant or employee if it would not impose an "undue hardship" on the operation of the employer's business. Undue hardship is defined as an action requiring significant difficulty or expense when considered in light of factors such as an employer's size, financial resources, and the nature and structure of its operation. An employer is not required to lower quality or production standards to make an accommodation; nor is an employer obligated to provide personal use items such as glasses or hearing aids.

CAN YOU ASK APPLICANTS ABOUT THEIR DISABILITIES?

An employer may not make a pre-employment inquiry on an application form or in an interview as to whether, or to what extent, an individual is disabled. The employer may ask a job applicant whether he or she can perform particular job functions. If the applicant has a disability known to the employer, the employer may ask how he or she can perform job functions that the employer considers difficult or impossible to perform because of the disability, and whether an accommodation would be needed.

CAN YOU REQUIRE MEDICAL EXAMINATIONS FOR APPLICANTS WITH DISABILITIES?

A job offer may be conditioned on the results of a medical examination, but only if the examination is required for all entering employees in similar jobs. Medical examinations of employees must be job related and consistent with the employer's business needs.

ARE APPLICANTS WHO USE ILLEGAL DRUGS COVERED BY THE ADA?

Employees and applicants currently engaging in the illegal use of drugs are not covered by the ADA when an employer acts on the basis of such use. Tests for illegal drugs are not subject to the ADA's restrictions on medical examinations. Employers may hold illegal drug users and alcoholics to the same performance standards as other employees.

WHAT IS UNLAWFUL RETALIATION?

It is also unlawful to retaliate against an individual for opposing employment practices that discriminate on the basis of disability or for filing a discrimination charge, testifying, or participating in any way in an investigation, proceeding, or litigation under the ADA.

WHO ENFORCES THE ADA?

The ADA is enforced by the Equal Employment Opportunity Commission (EEOC) and/or by state human rights agencies.

WHAT ARE THE COSTS OF LOSING AN ADA DISCRIMINATION CLAIM?

Remedies may include hiring, reinstatement, back pay, court orders to stop discrimination, and reasonable accommodation. Compensatory damages may be awarded for actual monetary losses and for future monetary losses, mental anguish, and inconvenience. Punitive damages may be available as well, if an employer acts with malice or reckless indifference. Attorney's fees may also be awarded.

EEOC DISABILITY CHARGE STATISTICS

In FY 2005, the EEOC received 14,893 charges of disability discrimination. They resolved 15,357 disability discrimination charges in FY 2005 and recovered $44.8 million in monetary benefits for charging parties and other aggrieved individuals (not including monetary benefits obtained through litigation).

Notes

INTRODUCTION

1. "Employment Facts about People with Disabilities in the United States," http://www.nod.org/index.cfm?fuseaction=page.viewPage&pageID=1430&nodeID=1&FeatureID=38&redirected=1&CFID=601394&CFTOKEN=62656341 (accessed September 29, 2006).

2. U.S. Census Bureau, "Definition of Disability Differs by Survey," http://www.census.gov/hhes/www/disability/disab_defn.html#ACS (accessed September 29, 2006).

3. Sheila D. Duston, "Definition of Disability Under the ADA: A Practical Overview and Update," http://www.ilr.cornell.edu/ped/hr_tips/article_1.cfm?b_id=27&view_all=true (accessed September 29, 2006); Herbert G. Heneman III and Timothy A. Judge, *Staffing Organizations* (Middleton, WI: Mendota House, 2006), 66–69.

4. Herbert G. Heneman III and Timothy A. Judge, *Staffing Organizations* (Middleton, WI: Mendota House, 2006), 66–69.

5. Sharon Stern and Mathew Brault, "Disability Data from the American Community Survey: A Brief Examination of the Effects of a Question Redesign in 2003," http://www.census.gov/hhes/www/disability/ACS_disability.pdf#search=%22american%20community%20survey%20definition%20of%20disability%203%20questions%22 (accessed October 4, 2006).

6. Judith Waldrop and Sharon M. Stern, "Disability Status 2000" (Washington, D.C.: U.S. Department of Commerce, Economics and Statistics Administration, U.S. Census Bureau, 2003).

7. "Employment Facts about People with Disabilities in the United States," http://www.nod.org/index.cfm?fuseaction=page.viewPage&pageID=1430&nodeID=1&FeatureID=38&redirected=1&CFID=601394&CFTOKEN=62656341 (accessed September 29, 2006).

8. "Employers Encouraged to Hire Qualified People with Disabilities," http://www.socialworkers.org/pressroom/2002/122302_earn.asp (accessed September 30, 2006).

9. "Studies Related to the Employment of Individuals with Disabilities" (1948–2000), http://oshkoshwdc.com/data/Studies_Related_to_the_Employment_of_Individuals_with_Disabilities.pdf#search=%22people%20with%20disabilities%20have%20lower%20absenteeism%20and%20turnover%22 (accessed September 30, 2006).

10. "Low Cost Accommodation Solutions," http://www.jan.wvu.edu/media/LowCostSolutions.html (accessed October 4, 2006).

11. Bob Peck and Lyn T. Kirkbride, "Why Businesses Don't Employ People with Disabilities," *Journal of Vocational Rehabilitation* 16, 71–75.

12. Secretary of Labor's New Freedom Initiative Award, http://www.dol.gov/odep/newfreedom/index.htm (accessed August 18, 2006).

CHAPTER 1

1. Jane Sneddon Little and Robert K. Triest, "The Impact of Demographic Change on U.S. Labor Markets," *Federal Reserve Bank of Boston New England Economic Review*, 2002 (First Quarter), 47–68.

2. Jane Sneddon Little and Robert K. Triest, "The Impact of Demographic Change," 47–68.

3. Mitra Toossi, "A Century of Change: The U.S. Labor Force, 1950-2050," *Monthly Labor Review*, 2002, 125(5):15–28.

4. Mitra Toossi, "A Century of Change," 15–28.

5. Mitra Toossi, "A Century of Change," 15–28.

6. Mitra Toossi, "A Century of Change," 15–28.

7. Mitra Toossi, "A Century of Change," 15–28.

8. Peter McDonald and Rebecca Kippen, "Labor Supply Prospects in 16 Developed Countries, 2000-2005," *Population and Development Review*, 2001, 27(1):1–32.

9. Jane Sneddon Little and Robert K. Triest, "The Impact of Demographic Change," 47–68.

10. R. Judy and C. D'Amico, *Workforce 2020: Work and Workers in the 21st Century* (Indianapolis, IN: Hudson Institute, 1997).

11. Jane Sneddon Little and Robert K. Triest, "The Impact of Demographic Change," 47–68.

12. Jane Sneddon Little and Robert K. Triest, "The Impact of Demographic Change," 47–68.

13. Peter McDonald and Rebecca Kippen, "Labor Supply Prospects," 1–32.

14. Rehabilitation Research and Training Center on Disability Demographics and Statistics, *2004 Disability Status Reports* (Ithaca, NY: Cornell University, 2005).

CHAPTER 2

1. Michael J. Millington, Edna M. Szymanski, and Cheryl Hanley-Maxwell, "Effect of the Label of Mental Retardation on Employer Concerns and Selection," *Rehabilitation Counseling Bulletin*, Vol. 38, No. 1 (1994): 27–43.

2. Rehabilitation Research and Training Center on Disability Demographics and Statistics, 2005 Disability Status Reports United States, Ithaca NY: Cornell University, http://www.ilr.cornell.edu/edi/disabilitystatistics/StatusReports/2005-pdf/2005-StatusReports_US.pdf?CFID=13413980&CFTOKEN=25087206 (accessed January 10, 2007)

3. Reed Greenwood and Virginia A. Johnson, "Employer Perspectives on Workers with Disabilities," *Journal of Rehabilitation*, Vol. 53, No. 3 (July–Sept 1987): 37–45.

4. Barbara A. Lee and Karen A. Newman, "Employer Responses to Disability: Preliminary Evidence and a Research Agenda," *Employee Responsibilities and Rights Journal*, Vol. 8, No. 3 (1995): 209–229.

5. Lloyd C. Junor, "Disabilities, Employers, and Employees: Some Issues," *Australian Journal of Social Issues*, Vol. 20 (1985): 295–307; Edward Yelin and Laura Trupin, "Successful Labor Market Transitions for Persons with Disabilities: Factors Affecting the Probability of Entering and Maintaining Employment," *Research in Social Science and Disability: Expanding the Scope of Social Science Research on Disability*, Vol. 1 (2000): 105–129.

6. Dean B. McFarlin, James Song, and Michelle Sonntag, "Integrating the Disabled into the Work Force: A Survey of Fortune 500 Company Attitudes and Practices," *Employee Responsibilities and Rights Journal*, Vol. 4, No. 4 (1991): 107–123.

7. Judith A. Cooke, Susan A. Pickett-Schenk, Dennis Grey, Michael Banghart, Robert A. Rosenheck, and Frances Randolph, "Vocational Outcomes among Formerly Homeless Persons with Severe Mental Illness in the ACCESS Program," *Psychiatric Services*, Vol. 52 (2001): 1075–1080; B. Coope, "Employment Potential of Persons with Mild Intellectual Impairments," *Canadian Journal of Rehabilitation*, Vol. 5 (1991): 81–92; R. Eigenbrood and P. Retish, "Work Experience: Employers' Attitudes Regarding the Employability of Special Education Students," *Career Development for Exceptional Individuals*, Vol. 11 (1988): 15–25; J. Kregel and Darlene Unger, "Employer Perceptions of the Work Potential of Individuals With Disabilities: An Illustration from Supported Employment," *Journal of Vocational Rehabilitation*, Vol. 3 (1993): 17–25; J. Nietupski, S. Hamre-Nietupski, N. S. VanderHart, and K. Fishback, "Employer Perceptions of the Benefits and Concerns of Supported Employment," *Education and Training in Mental Retardation and Developmental Disabilities*, Vol. 31 (1996): 310–323; D. M. Petty and E. M. Fussell, "Employer Attitudes and Satisfaction with Supported Employment. Focus on Autism and Other Developmental Disabilities," Vol. 12 (1997): 15–22; J. Sandys, "'It Does My Heart Good': The Perceptions of Employers Who Have Hired People with Intellectual Disabilities through Supported Employment Programs" (Doctoral dissertation, University of Toronto, 1993), *Dissertation Abstracts International*, Vol. 54 (1994): 3593; M. S. Shafer, J. Hill, J. Seyfarth, and P. Wehman, "Competitive Employment and Workers with Mental Retardation: Analysis of Employers' Perceptions and Experiences," *American Journal of Mental Retardation*, Vol. 3 (1987): 304–311; L. Wilgosh and H. H. Mueller, "Employer Attitudes toward Hiring Individuals with Mental Disabilities," *Canadian Journal of Rehabilitation*, Vol. 3 (1989): 43–47.

8. Gina A. Livermore, David C. Stapleton, Mark W. Nowak, David C. Wittenburg, and Elizabeth D. Eisman, *The Economics of Policies and Programs Affecting the*

Employment of People with Disabilities, Rehabilitation Research and Training Center for Economic Research on Employment Policy for Persons with Disabilities (2000), http://digitalcommons.ilr.cornell.edu/edicollect/79/. (accessed January 10, 2007)

9. Greenwood and Johnson, "Employer Perspectives on Workers with Disabilities," 37–45.

10. Michael.A. Stein, "Labor Markets, Rationality, and Workers with Disabilities," *Berkeley Journal of Employment and Labor Law*, Vol. 21, No. 1 (2000): 314–334.

11. Lee and Newman, "Employer Responses to Disability," 209–229.

12. McFarlin, Song, and Sonntag, "Integrating the Disabled into the Work Force," 107–123.

13. L. A. Blessing, and J. Jamieson, "Employing Persons with a Developmental Disability: Effects of Previous Experience," *Canadian Journal of Rehabilitation*, Vol. 12, No. 4 (1999): 211–21; S. C. Burnham, "Comparison of the Perceptions of Employers, Service Providers, and Educable Mentally Retarded/Learning-Disabled Students as Related to Successful Employment" (Doctoral dissertation, Mississippi State University, 1990), *Dissertation Abstracts International*, Vol. 52 (1991): 426; E. Diksa and E. S. Rogers, "Employer Concerns about Hiring Persons with Psychiatric Disability: Results of the Employer Attitude Questionnaire," *Rehabilitation Counseling Bulletin*, Vol. 40 (1996): 31–44; D. R. Fuqua, M. Rathburn, and E. M. Gade, "A Comparison of Employer Attitudes toward the Worker Problems of Eight Types of Disabilities," *Vocational Evaluation and Work Adjustment Bulletin*, Vol. 15, No. 1 (1984): 40–43; Virginia A. Johnson, Reed Greenwood, and K. F. Schriner, "Work Performance and Work Personality: Employer Concerns about Workers With Disabilities," *Rehabilitation Counseling Bulletin*, Vol. 32 (1988): 50–57; T. L. Scheid, "Employment of Individuals with Mental Disabilities: Business Response to the ADA's Challenge," Behavioral Sciences and the Law, Vol. 17 (1999): 73–91; G. R. Weisenstein and H. L. Koshman, "The Influence of Being Labeled Handicapped on Employer Perceptions of the Importance of Worker Traits for Successful Employment," *Career Development for Exceptional Individuals*, Vol. 14 (1991): 67–76.

14. Suzann Gaspar, "Disabled, Not Unable: In IT, a Disability Is no Liability," *Network World*, Vol. 17, No. 29 (July 17, 2000): 85.

15. Melissa Solomon, "Hiring the Invisible Workforce: Industry Trend or Event?" *Computerworld*, Vol. 34, No. 32 (August 7, 2000): 54.

16. K. E. Mitchell, G. M. Alliger, and R. Morfopoulos, "Toward an ADA-Appropriate Job Analysis," *Human Resource Management Review*, Vol. 7 (1997): 5–26.

17. Low Cost Accommodation Solutions, http://www.jan.wvu.edu/media/LowCostSolutions.html (accessed October 3, 2006).

18. M. L. Lengnick-Hall, Philip M. Gaunt, and Jessica Collison, *Employer Incentives for Hiring Individuals With Disabilities* (Alexandria, VA: Society for Human Resource Management, 2003).

19. Frederick C. Collignon, "The Role of Reasonable Accommodation in Employing Disabled Persons in Private Industry," in Monroe Berkowitz and M. Anne Hill (eds.), *Disability and the Labor Market: Economic Problems, Policies, and Programs*

(Ithaca, NY: ILR Press, 1986): 196–241; Lee and Newman, "Employer Responses to Disability," 209–229.

20. Dennis Gilbride, Robert Stensrud, Connie Ehlers, Eric Evans, and Craig Peterson, "Employers' Attitudes toward Hiring Persons with Disabilities and Vocational Rehabilitation Services," *Journal of Rehabilitation*, Vol. 66, No. 4 (Oct–Dec 2000): 17–23; Terry J. Moore and William Crimando, "Attitudes Toward Title I of the Americans with Disabilities Act," *Rehabilitation Counseling Bulletin*, Vol. 38, No. 3 (1995): 232–247; R. Roessler and G. Sumner, "Employer Opinions about Accommodating Employees with Chronic Illness," *Journal of Applied Rehabilitation Counseling*, Vol. 28 (1997): 29–34; S. Walters and C. Baker, "Title I of the Americans with Disabilities Act: Employer and recruiter attitudes toward individuals with disabilities," *Journal of Rehabilitation Administration*, Vol. 20, No. 1 (1996): 15–23.

21. John T. Hazer and Karen V. Bedell, "Effects of Seeking Accommodation and Disability on Preemployment Evaluations," *Journal of Applied Social Psychology*, Vol. 30, No. 6 (2000): 1201–23.

22. Marcie Pitt-Catsouphes and John Butterworth, *Different Perspectives: Workplace Experience with the Employment of Individuals with Disabilities* (Rehabilitation Research and Training Center, 1995, http://eric.ed.gov/ERICWebPortal/Home.portal?_nfpb= true&_pageLabel=RecordDetails&ERICExtSearch_SearchValue_0=ED411623& ERICExtSearch_SearchType_0=eric_accno&objectId=0900000b801219b4 (accessed January 10, 2007); "Promoting the Employment of Individuals with Disabilities," Institute for Community Inclusion at Children's Hospital Center on Work and Family at Boston University.

23. "Studies Related to the Employment of Individuals with Disabilities (1948–2000)," http://oshkoshwdc.com/data/Studies_Related_to_the_Employment_of_ Individuals_with_Disabilities.pdf#search=%22studies%20related%20to%20the% 20employment%20of%20people%20with%20disabilities%22 (accessed October 3, 2006).

24. Lengnick-Hall, Gaunt, and Collison, *Employer Incentives for Hiring Individuals With Disabilities*.

25. Daron Acemoglu and Joshua D. Angrist, "Consequences of Employment Protection? The Case of the Americans with Disabilities Act," *The Journal of Political Economy*, Vol. 109, No. 5 (Oct 2001): 915–57.

26. Amy Allbright, "2001 Employment Decisions under the ADA Title 1—Survey Update," *Mental and Physical Disability Law Reporter, ABA*, http://www.abanet.org/ disability/reporter/feature.html (accessed October 5, 2006); Barbara A. Lee, "The Implications of ADA Litigation for Employers: A Review of Federal Appellate Court Decisions," *Human Resource Management*, Vol. 40, No. 1 (2001): 35–50.

27. Greenwood and Johnson, "Employer Perspectives on Workers with Disabilities," 37–45.

28. Dianna Stone and Adrienne Colella, "A Model of Factors Affecting the Treatment of Disabled Individuals in Organizations," *Academy of Management Review*, Vol. 21, No. 2 (1996): 352–402.

29. Adrienne Colella, Angelo S. DeNisi, and Arup Varma, "The Impact of Ratee's Disability on Performance Judgments and Choice as Partner: The Role of Disability-job Fit Stereotypes and Interdependence of Rewards," *Journal of Applied Psychology*, Vol. 83, No. 1 (1998): 102–111.

30. Adrienne Colella, "Coworker Distributive Fairness Judgments of the Work-place Accommodation of Employees with Disabilities," *Academy of Management Review*, Vol. 26, No. 1 (2001): 100–116.

31. "Expanding Your Market: Customers with Disabilities Mean Business," http://www.usdoj.gov/crt/ada/busstat.htm (accessed October 3, 2006).

CHAPTER 3

1. Hewlett Packard New Freedom Initiative Award Nomination document (un-dated).

2. Personal communication, June 23, 2005.

3. Sid Reel, personal communication, June 23, 2005.

4. Marleen Sloper, personal communication, June 23, 2005.

5. Bill Tipton, personal communication, June 23, 2005.

6. Bill Tipton, personal communication, June 23, 2005.

7. Bill Tipton, personal communication, June 23, 2005.

8. Bill Tipton, personal communication, June 23, 2005.

9. Michael Takemura, personal communication, June 23, 2005.

10. Michael Takemura, personal communication, June 23, 2005.

11. Michael Takemura, personal communication, June 23, 2005.

12. Sid Reel, personal communication, June 23, 2005.

CHAPTER 4

1. www.dow.com/careers/what/awd_amsoc.htm (accessed October 3, 2006).

2. R. Herman, T. Olivo, and J. Gioia, *Impending Crisis: Too Many Jobs, Too Few People* (Winchester, VA: Oakhill Press, 2003).

3. Kathy McDonald, personal communication, June 15, 2005.

4. Equal Employment Opportunity Commission, 2001 EEO-1 Aggregate Report: SIC 281: Industrial Organic Chemicals, www.eeoc.gov/stats/jobpat/2001/sic3/281.html (accessed October 5, 2006).

5. Kathy McDonald, personal communication, June 15, 2005.

6. Kathy McDonald, personal communication, June 15, 2005.

7. www.dow.com/careers/what/hr_option.htm (accessed October 3, 2006).

8. Kathy McDonald, personal communication, June 15, 2005.

9. Kathy McDonald, personal communication, June 15, 2005.

10. Kathy McDonald, personal communication, June 15, 2005.

11. www.dow.com/careers/why/network.htm (accessed October 3, 2006).

12. Kathy McDonald, personal communication, June 15, 2005.

13. 2000 Citation for Six Sigma, American Society for Training & Development. www.dow.com/careers/what/awd_amsoc.htm (accessed August 26, 2006).

14. Kathy McDonald, personal communication, June 15, 2005.

15. Kathy McDonald, personal communication, June 15, 2005.

16. Kathy McDonald, personal communication, June 15, 2005.

17. Kathy McDonald, personal communication, June 15, 2005.

18. Kathy McDonald, personal communication, June 15, 2005.

19. www.dow.com/commitments/responsibility/policies (accessed October 4, 2006).

20. Kathy McDonald, personal communication, June 15, 2005.

21. Kathy McDonald, personal communication, June 15, 2005.

22. http://dow.com/careers (accessed October 4, 2006).

23. http://dow.com/careers (accessed October 4, 2006).

CHAPTER 5

1. SunTrust Banks, Inc., SunTrust in Brief,http://301url.com/34k (accessed June 17, 2006).

2. Katherine McCary, personal communication, June 22, 2005.

3. Katherine McCary, personal communication, June 22, 2005; SunTrust, 2006.

4. Katherine McCary, personal communication, June 22, 2005; Stephanie Overman, "Winning Ways," *HR Magazine*, Vol. 45, No. 7 (2000), http://www.shrm.org/hrmagazine/2000inex/0700/0700overman.asp (accessed June 13, 2006).

5. United States Department of Labor, SunTrust Banks, Inc, http://www.dol.gov/odep/newfreedom/nfi03.htm#geinc (accessed July 15, 2005).

6. United States Department of Labor, SunTrust Banks, Inc., http://www.dol.gov/odep/newfreedom/nfi03.htm#geinc (accessed July 15, 2005).

7. United States Department of Labor, SunTrust Banks, Inc., http://www.dol.gov/odep/newfreedom/nfi03.htm#geinc (accessed July 15, 2005).

8. Katherine McCary, personal communication, June 22, 2005.

9. United States Department of Labor, SunTrust Banks, Inc., http://www.dol.gov/odep/newfreedom/nfi03.htm#geinc (accessed July 15, 2005).

10. United States Department of Labor, SunTrust Banks, Inc., http://www.dol.gov/odep/newfreedom/nfi03.htm#geinc (accessed July 15, 2005).

11. Katherine McCary, personal communication, June 22, 2005.

CHAPTER 7

1. Dale Giovengo, personal communication, June 2005; United States Department of Labor, Giant Eagle Inc., http://www.dol.gov/odep/newfreedom/nfi03.htm#geinc (accessed June 15, 2005).

2. Giant Eagle, "Traditions of Success," http://www.gianteagle.com/main/article7.jsp?CONTENT%3C%3Ecnt_id=1110261&FOLDER%3C%3Efolder_id=1110257&bmUID=1150723449711 (accessed June 15, 2005).

3. United States Department of Labor, Giant Eagle Inc., http://www.dol.gov/odep/newfreedom/nfi03.htm#geinc (accessed June 15, 2005).

4. Dale Giovengo, personal communication, June 2005.

5. Dale Giovengo, personal communication, June 2005.

6. United States Department of Labor, Giant Eagle, Inc., http://www.dol.gov/odep/newfreedom/nfi03.htm#geinc (accessed June 15, 2005).

7. United States Department of Labor, Giant Eagle Inc., http://www.dol.gov/odep/newfreedom/nfi03.htm#geinc (accessed June 15, 2005).

8. United States Department of Labor, Giant Eagle Inc., http://www.dol.gov/odep/newfreedom/nfi03.htm#geinc (accessed June 15, 2005).

9. Dale Giovengo, personal communication, June 2005.

10. Dale Giovengo, personal communication, June 2005.

11. Dale Giovengo, personal communication, June 2005.

CHAPTER 8

1. United States Department of Labor, New Freedom Initiative Award Application, Microsoft.

2. United States Department of Labor, New Freedom Initiative Award Application, Microsoft.

CHAPTER 9

1. www.marriott.com; www.marriottfoundation.org (accessed October 5, 2006).

2. J. M. Williams, "A Chat with Richard Marriott," *Business Week* (September 22, 1999); http://www.businessweek.com/bwdaily/dnflash/sep1999/nf90922d.htm (accessed August 16, 2006).

3. About Bridges, http://marriottfoundation.org/foundation/facts.mi (accessed August 16, 2006).

4. Sue Weber, personal communication, June 16, 2005.

5. Sue Weber, personal communication, June 16, 2005.

6. "Marriott Training Investment Yields Exemplary Employees," http://www.earnworks.com/Success_Stories/marriott.htm (accessed October 5, 2006).

7. Sue Weber, personal communication, June 16, 2005.

8. Sue Weber, personal communication, June 16, 2005.

9. Sue Weber, personal communication, June 16, 2005.

10. Sue Weber, personal communication, June 16, 2005.

11. Sue Weber, personal communication, June 16, 2005.

12. Sue Weber, personal communication, June 16, 2005.

CHAPTER 10

1. BLS Releases 2004-14 Employment Projections, http://www.bls.gov/news.release/ecopro.nr0.htm (accessed September 26, 2006).

2. Wayne F. Cascio, *Costing Human Resources: The Financial Impact of Behavior in Organizations* (Cincinnati, OH: South-Western College Publishing, 2000)

3. "Private Employer Business Case," http://www.earnworks.com/Private_Employers/pbc/retention.htm (accessed September 26, 2006); R. Greenwood and V. A. Johnson, "Employer Perspectives on Workers with Disabilities," *Journal of Rehabilitation*, Vol. 53 (1987): 37–44; R. A. Lester and D. W. Caudill, "The Handicapped Worker: Seven Myths," *Training and Development Journal*, Vol. 41 (1987): 50–51; Wendy S. Parent and J. M Everson, "Competencies of Disabled Workers in Industry: A Review of Business Literature," *Journal of Rehabilitation*, Vol. 52, No. 4 (1986): 16–23; G. E. Stevens, "Exploding the Myths about Hiring the Handicapped," *Personnel*, Vol. 63 (1986): 57–60.

4. Patrick Wright, S. P. Ferris, J. S. Hiller, and M. Kroll, "Competitiveness through Management of Diversity: Effects on Stock Price Valuation," *Academy of Management Journal*, Vol. 38 (1995): 272–287.

5. "About AAPD," http://www.aapd-dc.org/docs/info.html (accessed October 5, 2006).

6. Lindsey Gerdes, "Get Ready for a Pickier Workforce: Today's Teens Say Employers without a Social Conscience Need Not Apply," *Business Week*, Vol. 82 (September 18, 2006).

7. "What Marketers Should Know about People with Disabilities," http://www.nod.org/index.cfm?fuseaction=page.viewPage&pageID=1430&nodeID=1&FeatureID=723&redirected=1&CFID=601394&CFTOKEN=62656341 (accessed September 26, 2006).

8. "Expanding Your Market: Customers with Disabilities Mean Business," http://www.usdoj.gov/crt/ada/busstat.htm (accessed October 5, 2006).

9. Susan E. Jackson, K. E. May, and K. Whitney, "Understanding the Dynamics of Diversity in Decision-Making Teams," in Richard Guzzo, Eduardo Salas, and Associates (eds.), *Team Effectiveness and Decision Making in Organizations* (San Francisco, CA: Jossey Bass, 1995).

10. John M. Williams, "Cisco Beats a Path to Disabled Workers: The High Tech Giant Has Seen the Good Business Sense of Scouting for Hires in the Disabled Community," http://www.businessweek.com/bwdaily/dnflash/jan2001/nf20010118_432.htm (accessed September 26, 2006).

11. Gary N. Siperstein, Neil Romano, Amanda Mohler, and Robin Parker, "A National Survey of Consumer Attitudes towards Companies That Hire People with Disabilities," *Journal of Vocational Rehabilitation*, Vol. 24, No. 1 (2006): 3–9.

12. Wright, Ferris, Hiller, and Kroll, "Competitiveness through management of diversity," 272–287.

CHAPTER 11

1. Benjamin Schneider, Sarah K. Gunnarson, and Kathryn Niles-Jolly, "Creating the climate and culture of success," *Organizational Dynamics*, Vol. 23, No. 1 (1994): 17–29.

2. James Charles Collins and Jerry I. Porras, *Built to Last: Successful Habits of Visionary Companies* (New York: Harper Business, 1994).

3. Benjamin Schneider, Arthur P. Brief, and Richard A. Guzzo, "Creating a Climate and Culture for Sustainable Organizational Change," *Organizational Dynamics*, 24(4) (1996): 6–19.

4. Schneider, Gunnarson, and Niles-Jolly, "Creating the Climate and Culture of Success," 17–29.

5. Sanford Jacoby, *Employing Bureaucracy: Managers, Unions, and the Transformation of Work in the 20th Century* (Mahwah, NJ: Erlbaum, 2004).

6. Kurt Lewin, *Field Theory in Social Science* (New York: Harper and Row, 1951); a summary of this theory can be found at http://www.mindtools.com/pages/article/newPPM_94.htm.

7. Edgar Schein, *Organizational Culture and Leadership*, 2nd ed. (San Francisco: Jossey-Bass, 1992).

8. Lewin's Change Management Model: Understanding the Three Stages of Change, http://www.mindtools.com/pages/article/newPPM_94.htm (accessed September 17, 2006).

9. Robert Rodgers, John E. Hunter, and Deborah L. Rogers, "Influence of Top Management Commitment on Management Program Success," *Journal of Applied Psychology*, Vol. 78, No. 1 (1993): 151–155.

10. Karl E. Weick, "Small Wins: Redefining the Scale of Social Problems," *American Psychologist*, Vol. 39, No. 1 (1984): 40–49.

11. Richard S. Allen and Kendyl A. Montgomery, "Applying an Organizational Development Approach to Creating Diversity," *Organizational Dynamics*, Vol. 30, No. 2 (2001): 149–161.

Index